AF192388

Walter van Laack

GREATER THAN
THE ENTIRE UNIVERSE

Author

Prof. Dr. med. Walter van Laack

Specialist for Orthopaedics and Orthopaedic Surgery,
Physiotherapy, Sports Medicine, Chiropractic and Acupuncture.
Author of numerous books for existential and natural philosophy

Book Cover

Designed by my son Martin van Laack, M.Sc.
Master of Science in Architecture (RWTH-Aachen, Germany)

Translation

Translated by Anneliese Wolstenholme, Roetgen near Aachen/Germany
from the original German "GRÖSSER ALS DAS GANZE UNIVERSUM", published 2021.
Once more I thank her very much for her very kind and patient cooperation.

The German edition was published 2021 in memory of my father

© 2022 by Prof. Dr. Walter van Laack
van Laack Buchverlag, D-Aachen
www.vanLaack-Buch.de   -   www.van-Laack.de
www.Nahtoderfahrung.info

Printing & Distribution by Books-on-Demand (BoD)
In de Tarpen 42, D-22848 Norderstedt; Fax +49-40-53433584
info@bod.de   -   www.bod.de

All rights reserved. This publication may not be reproduced in whole or in part by printing, phono or photomechanical reproduction, photo copying, microfilming, computer processing, transfer to the internet and translation or any other means of recording and reproducing by existing and future media. Exceptions only with the prior written permission by the author or the publisher.

ISBN 978-3-936624-52-6

Contents

Part 1: The Alpha and the Omega

Born during the Cologne Carnival

On 10th November 2009 the former goal keeper of the German Soccer league Hannover 96 committed suicide due to a severe depression. Throughout Germany people were deeply shocked. The befriended Catholic deacon and cabaret artist Willibert Pauels, then still active as carnival speaker during the Cologne Carnival under his stage name „Ne Bergische Jung", referred to this tragic event in a very compassionate way in one of his speeches. He wanted to demonstrate that the Cologne Carnival can also show a completely different and very contemplative aspect.

In addressing a large audience he said: *"Do you know what touches me most of all deep inside in view of this dreadful matter? It was what Mrs Enke did the day after the tragic death of her husband. She went to her daughter Lara's grave, who died when she was two years old, and she put up a sign which said only a few words: And these few words say it all! She had written: LARA, DADDY IS COMING!"*

He then went on: *"And that is what counts: When I am able to have this perspective, that no death, no illness, no depression, no abyss in this world can destroy our souls; since they are LARGER THAN THE ENTIRE UNIVERSE!"*

Willibert Pauels gave his consent for this book to carry this title. And in my opinion he is absolutely right.

Our world is wonderful and, in fact, possibly much more magnificent than we can at all imagine with our narrow minds. Unfortunately, many of us are not at all prepared to recognise this.

In 1999 I published my first very detailed book „*Plädoyer für ein Leben nach dem Tod und eine etwas andere Sicht der Welt*"[1] ("Pleading for life after death and a somewhat different view of our world", published in German only).

---

[1] See bibliographical information on my book list at the end of this book

Even then it was quite clear to me: Our path "here on Earth" is only the beginning and probably only a small part of a journey which is a long one for all of us and, in spite of many findings and insights, a journey into the unknown. Each and every one of us will be allowed – and indeed must – follow this path and that means going far beyond what we call our "death" in the "Here and Now".

Such a notion did not correspond to the state of scientific knowledge in 1999, it did not then and neither does it today. Even today, (supposedly) "enlightened human beings" shy away from adhering to such a conviction, lest they provoke personal disadvantages – especially at work.

I questioned this "state of scientific knowledge", which is still standard today, very critically early on and my conclusion was the same back then as it is today: Most of the cosmological and –theoretical explanations of existence are not very credible upon closer inspection.

In most cases they are interpretations of observations, measurements and phenomena which do indeed actually occur but which are then interpreted in accordance with the spirit of the time – the zeitgeist. Whereupon purely speculative hypotheses are then built, which in turn simply ignore quite different, but probably also true, observations and many other phenomena because they do not correspond to the zeitgeist.

Today, more than twenty years and numerous books later, my fundamental conviction, which has grown over more than forty years, remains unchanged. On the contrary, it has become an even stronger conviction.

We all practically resemble small ants moving around within a very limited part of the real world. Meanwhile we do seem to be equipped with what we consider to be a respectable intellectual competence. Unfortunately this tempts many people to assume a somewhat adolescent arrogance which distances them from reality instead of drawing them closer to it. Therefore, I dare once again here to claim firmly: *There is no death, but simply life for a life that has come into existence.*

And above all there is a higher "entity" which is completely incomprehensible for us humans, which will probably forever elude any description by humans and which we here simply call "God", for example.

We can approach "him+her" to some extent only in a very rudimentary way. However, this is exactly what we ought to do, since from this approach and from the clear convictions developing from there, great responsibility arises for each and every one of us in the "here and now", which we must assume as early and as comprehensively as possible.

We must all learn this now, each one of us individually.

So, this is important for each individual and I will come back to this later. Some people may want to claim now that I am close to being an utter nutcase. They are free to do so. Everyone should and must decide for themselves whether they want to stop reading now or whether they are prepared to open their minds to this subject now with which they will be confronted sooner or later anyway.

There is true religiosity in all of these reflections. However, it has little in common with the religions and myths which have developed in the course of human history and the religious institutions based thereon and their ideals, which are often restrictive or even punitive. The very essence of true religiosity is highly liberating, but it also requires "cooperation".

What does Soul mean?

The word "soul" corresponds with the ancient Greek word "psyche". According to this, it can be understood as the entirety of a person's feeling, perception and thought. Thus it is not fixed and it keeps growing incessantly, thereby maturing individually in each living being. The soul is the sum of all spiritual characteristics and personality traits of individual human beings at any point in their lives.

According to present understanding the soul also possesses *transcendental* elements. It is considered to be the insubstantial and

6

intangible part of human beings which, according to numerous religious beliefs, lives on after death, i.e. it is immortal. The ancient Greeks did not yet perceive any transcendental elements in souls.

Some religious and philosophical concepts thus see the soul as an "immaterial" (spiritual) principle which is also considered to be the bearer of the actual life of human beings and their lifelong continual identities.

Other concepts even assume that its soul already existed before an individual came to life, that a "living being" is merely a kind of temporary manifestation of this soul. For them, death is the process of separating the soul from the body it "inhabited" until then, with the aim of returning in a new, different, physical body after a certain "length of stay" (belief in reincarnation; more on this later).

Grave goods, burial rites as well as numerous wall and cave paintings, enable us to assume quite safely that human beings have always been convinced of *"three core theses"* since time immemorial. I believe they are also part of the universal principles of human incarnation such as the awareness (Hebrew: *"Tardemah"*) of human procreation, misrepresented as the creation of Eve from Adam's rib (Old Testament, Genesis 2)[2].

These three core theses are probably also the crucial "three common denominators" of all religions and myths. They are all based on these denominators in one way or another, even if the respective interpretations and the narratives, stories and legends circulating around them are very diverse. Without these "three common denominators" all religions and myths would be *worthless.* This applies in particular to the third point below:

1) There is an existence which is superior to us humans in all respects. We cannot even come close to describing it adequately. Some speak of a "Power of Creation" (see Bible, Old Testament, Genesis 1, in Hebrew

---

[2] The awareness of human procreation seems to be behind the real meaning of the story about Adam's "rib". The Hebrew word „zelo" means above all "bow", formerly a euphemism of the shamefully never mentioned word "penis" ...

„*Elohim*") or simply of "Creation". Others speak of a "Divine Dimension" covering a wide spectrum of deities or gods in ancient traditions. The more recent monotheistic religions refer to it as "God" or "Allah". I myself also prefer these "singular" formulations, since from our perspective it must be a higher and completely indescribable *"entity"*. The force behind it is beyond our description and understanding.

Even if the current zeitgeist strictly rejects and dismisses such ideas; they are directly intertwined with the emerging of mankind. And I believe that early humans were thus closer to the truth than many today, in our supposedly enlightened age.

2) There is a second reality which we can perceive and which is perceptible in us. This can also be experienced, but not "sensually"; for it is not of a physical nature. From our perspective, it is "immaterial" and thus also the basis for the belief in a human "soul".

This second reality can also be described as the "spiritual level", the "land of souls" or, in general, the "spiritual dimension". All human beings are already part of *both* dimensions during their lifetime. With their "physical deaths" they "survive" on this second level.

3) From this, the third core-element of these deep convictions, which have grown since the beginning of mankind, follows inevitably: The death of each individual human being can only be of a physical nature. The soul survives it directly. Only in the course of time did the emerging religions "shape" the most diverse "survival models" thereof.

Recent experiments clearly indicate that the belief in the survival of death – in whatever form – even seems to be fundamentally inherent in humans:

In 2008, the US psychologist *Jesse Bering* presented a play to primary school children at *Belfast University in Ireland* in which a mouse is eaten by a crocodile. He then asked the children about the fate of the mouse. They all were of the opinion that with death, the physical functions of the mouse had ceased. But they were also sure that its soul continued to exist.

This answer was given by pupils up to the age of about 12, irrespective of whether they had grown up in a religious family home or not.

Already in 1999, while comparing 104 fraternal and 169 identical twins, other researchers at the University of Minnesota in the USA had already found that – similar to intelligence and musical abilities – religiosity is also likely to be a "genetic" predisposition independent of environment, upbringing and culture.

However, there seems to be no "gene" for this actually, even if some contemporaries claim that there is. This disposition is not biochemical in nature. People speak here of "epigenetic influences", without knowing exactly what they really mean by this.

The current zeitgeist just speaks a completely different language:

As a rule, the leading media spread the idea that in fact only matter can really exist. We therefore talk about the age of materialism or naturalism. Because it is assumed that we can *reduce* everything to physical matter, this is also referred to as reductionism. Mere "information" or, generally speaking, everything "informational" also exists, of course, although not in reality but only in "our head" (i.e. in the brain) and thus only if it is connected with matter.

Hence, it is generally firmly believed today that "our spirit" is merely a "product" of our brain. In this context, philosophers also talk of "epiphenomena".

This means, of course, that the soul also only exists as long as the body or its brain, as the physical medium of the soul, is alive. When humans (or animals) die, their souls could no longer exist. Such ideas become dangerous, in my opinion, when some contemporaries want to establish a connection between a human brain and technical devices, e.g. modern computers, and then think that they could achieve "eternal life" by transferring a brain-linked spirit to a machine. They believe that with the aid of "artificial intelligence" (AI) they could create new and advanced beings in a human-operated "evolution" for whom death would perhaps be unknown. The term "transhumanism", where the brain is connected to a machine, has been haunting the media for a long time now. Such a development would probably also have the effect that some people or their "trans-humanistic avatars" could be monitored or even strategically controlled for the requirements of just a few who like to consider themselves to be the elite. For some, such appalling models seem to be in vogue today, especially in the context of the pandemic spread of the "Covid-19" virus. In fact, in 2020, numerous "political intentions" already seem to have departed from a medically plausible basis of this pandemic.[3]

Of course, these entirely naturalistic convictions also apply to all questions concerning a superior entity and a higher level which is utterly indescribable for us and which is called "God" in Christianity or "Allah" in Islam.

Thus, the German magazine "Der Spiegel" once again gave us a "lecture" in its issue no. 24 published 7th June 2014 with its elaborate editorial *"Das unsterbliche Gerücht"* (The Immortal Rumour) stating that, of course, there is no "God".

Even the very idea, they said, was naïve and no longer in tune with our age of enlightened science. Thus, the cover of this issue was also meant to be ironic, when it said "Is anyone there?", subtitled "The Future of Religion: Faith without God".

For many people the articles of such magazines are downright "dogmas" since they claim to be based on scientific findings.

Many contemporaries remain unswervingly loyal even if later many of these editorials turn out to be lies or entirely or to a large extent fictitious.

In a TV programme, moderated by *(Gert) Scobel* on the German TV station 3SAT, broadcast in 2008, *Professor Günter Hasinger,* at the time plasma physicist at the Max-Planck-Institute in Garching near Munich, Germany, pointed out explicitly that *"a dilemma in physics"* indeed exists; due to a law of nature, applying to all physical matter, which states that order decreases steadily while disorder steadily increases ($\approx$entropy).

---

[3] See also Klaus Schwab's book "The Great Reset", published in July 2020. Professor Schwab is the founder of the World Economic Forum (WEF), where renowned politicians and numerous leaders of major economic groups meet on an annual basis in Davos, Switzerland.

On the other hand, however, some features of crucial importance such as our brain, for example, show simultaneously that "information" or, in general everything "informational", continues to grow.

Hence, it is easy to recognise that in our world there must be two sides of one and the same coin which are mirror images of each other and simultaneously opposites. I term them "polar-symmetrical".

Even the ancient Chinese philosophers Lao-tse and Kung-fu-tse had already recognised this 2500 years ago to be a generally valid law of nature and had described it in a unique way with the symbol of Yin und Yang (see Fig. 1)

Fig. 1: Yin and Yang

In all finite, i.e. physical or material bodies in the entire universe, *disorder* is constantly increasing: Thus suns and planets evolve, they grow in the course of millions or even billions of years until they reach their zenith before they perish again and disintegrate millions or even billions of years later. This circular *(cyclical)* course applies to everything.

We too are born; we grow up and become adults after about 20 years. However, from the age of 30 onwards the human body starts to decline relentlessly and strives in a *cyclical* process towards its physical death. Everything in physics is subject to this growing disorder, this *entropy.*

However, there exists – just as consistently – a counterpart:

All *information* increases steadily. Everything *"informational"* has a straight *(linear)* and ascending course. This leads inevitably to the question as to whether and, if so, how, can something which continues to grow and multiply until the physical death of a human being – i.e. the "informational core", the real personality or the constantly "maturing soul" – continues to exist even when the body – and thus also the brain – disintegrates?

Does this mean that information, everything "informational" in this world, is just as *"really existent"* as all human bodies, all planets or suns in the entire universe, just like "matter"?

11

And is all the "informational", is information perhaps the "actual reality behind the reality of matter"?

Then we should also ask how we could best approach a plausible and well-founded answer to these questions.

In the first part of the book "The Alpha and the Omega" the essential basics and interconnections are shown and a clear answer is given to the question as to whatever could be "greater than the entire universe". We will further delve into all these conceptions and will clarify individual interconnections in the second part "Insights and Backgrounds".

Subjective Approaches

Since the end of the 1970s, I have been preoccupied with the subject of death and the question, which is sure to be very much in the mind of every human being at some time or other: Is there perhaps an *"After"*?

While I was without doubt a "Saul", i.e. someone who rejected and dismissed such things as naïve, just like it is still fashionable in the modern zeitgeist, I have long since become a "Paul".

Today I am utterly convinced that an "After" exists and I not only consider it as a given fact but even as a necessity.

Many people experience very unique incidents in the course of their lives – due to a wide variety of circumstances and situations – after which they often say that "something strange was afoot". For these experiences I once coined the term "out-of-body experiences of consciousness", OBEC for short. I, too, have had some such experiences, and some of them have not been merely exhilarating. There have also been cases when they were helpful and very important for my further life. Moreover, there have been cases where I should have paid more attention – thus avoiding some tragic developments.

OBECs are, in most cases, purely subjective experiences without a *clear cause-and-effect relationship.* These would than be classified as random parallel events, so-called *coincidences*. This can rarely be dismissed, since causalities can only be conclusively verified in very few cases.

Nevertheless, they seem to exist – and then they should perhaps be investigated and not just notoriously ignored as happens in most cases.

OBECs are probably much more common than many may think. According to some estimates it seems that a fifth up to even a quarter of all people have such experiences in the course of their lives.

Most people ignore them, dismiss them as coincidence and, by all means, they avoid talking about them, even with friends and partners. Probably with some justification they believe that they will be "looked at askance" at least, or, too quickly, even considered as being mentally ill, since they seem to be hallucinating and they would probably not be entirely wrong in their perception.

The most known and today best analysed OBECs are "near-death-experiences (NDEs)". Much more common, however, are so-called "after-death-contacts (ADCs)" – a rather unfortunate term:

During NDEs, people have spiritual experiences on the verge of their own, possibly imminent death, e.g. at the scene of an accident or, more often nowadays, while lying on an operating table during an often serious operation with complications.

ADCs, on the other hand, are experienced by many people in the immediate temporal proximity to the death of a beloved relative, partner or friend. However, it is not uncommon for them to occur many months later. The more time elapses the less frequently ADCs occur.[4]

The occurrence of NDEs is mostly explained by hallucinations, oxygen deficiency and endogenous opiates or with externally administered medication. However, NDEs are not the subject of this book. All I would like to point out here is that all these arguments can at best only partially explain NDEs, and even then the explanations remain unsatisfactory. Yet, many contents, such as universal patterns and especially out-of-body experiences (OBEs) with long since dead people, defy all attempts at explanation. This applies especially when those

---

[4] See also: Elsaesser, Evelyn, "Nachtod Kontakte" (After-death-contacts), new edition Crotona (2020)

affected (or better: blessed) often change their individual lifestyle significantly after having gone through such an experience.

A very important aspect, however, concerns both NDEs and ADCs and many other OBECs: If we are intensively pursuing the subject of such experiences then we will now and again meet people whose experience lay completely beyond their possible horizon of experience while they encountered it. In other words: At that moment, it was impossible for the person who experienced and witnessed these events to experience and to witness them. After all, they were lying on an operating table under general anaesthetic, for example, and thus were unable to see anything happening around them. But everything happened verifiably in the same room at exactly that time – or in some cases even outside the operating theatre.

Such moments make these subjects extremely fascinating and still, these events are likely to be deliberately ignored by numerous sceptics despite their having been verified and objectified in many cases after the event.

In this respect, NDEs and ADCs and other moments of spiritual experiences not only offer a huge source of narratives, most of which are to be taken seriously and very often have similar contents and patterns. No, in addition they often describe situations the experience of which could be objectively confirmed later.

Therefore, even the cautious approach to such subjective patterns of experience offers many useful and helpful arguments for the assumption that information or, in general terms, the informational as such, must not necessarily be attached to physical bodies as we know and perceive them with our senses. However, this purely "subjective approach" alone is, of course, not really conclusive proof in a more "scientific sense".

Objective Approaches

First of all, the question arises as to whether the "soul" of a human being (or that of an animal, for they are also "informationally growing

14

beings"), which according to my definition represents the entire personality of a person at the moment of death, must at all be considered as "bodiless" at the moment of death.

Esotericism knows the term "ethereal body". All physicists will, of course, roll their eyes now, but is this really justified? I will come back to this later.

For now, I just speculate that it is exactly like this: The "soul" of the being who has just died is not completely bodiless in death; it rather possesses a kind of "ethereal body".

Numerous people who experience (or are lucky to experience)[5] an NDE while they are close to death, may see themselves lying at the scene of an accident or on the operating table. Afterwards, they are often able to describe precisely what had happened to them or around them during this often very short period of time. They mostly even state to never having been as clear and oriented as during that situation.

And they say that, without any doubt, they perceived themselves as being "complete". Of course, they were irritated that "down there" they could see their own damaged body while attempts were being made to resuscitate them. And yet, according to their own statements, they felt like the same "I" as before and even seemed to have the same "body" which could hardly be right. This alone suggests that our "worldly" (sensual) perception of physical bodies could also be rather selective and biased.

Three examples may make this a bit easier to understand

1) Let us consider a caterpillar and a butterfly. The caterpillar is (in principle) a being in a world limited and attuned to two-dimensionality, even though it can crawl up plants into the three-dimensionality of space. Nevertheless, it does not have the "perception" of a three-dimensional space as we know it: Even though it is "climbing up", this

---

[5] Alois Serwaty, the founder and long-time President of the German Network "Nahtoderfahrung" (Near-death Experience (N.NTE)), a near-death expert himself, whom I hold in very high esteem, talked of "blessed persons".

remains a two-dimensional process – assuming here, of course, that in theory "its spirit" would be capable of doing so at all.

Eventually, one day the caterpillar will turn into a butterfly.

From then on, it will be able to experience three-dimensional space with all its new possibilities and at the same time it will no longer take any notice of caterpillars. Let us assume that it could perceive all this with a kind of "rudimentary consciousness": Surely though it will still lack any "memory" of its previous life as a caterpillar and the comparative limitation relating to its former two-dimensional life. In the same way, a caterpillar will not "recognise and perceive" the butterfly, since it is now escaping into the three-dimensional space. In its own "horizon of understanding", the caterpillar is still completely unaware of this new dimension.

Applying these principles to humans, we could imagine that at the moment of death there is an immediate change of dimension for our "soul". This is the result of the human personality growing up to this moment of "death". In some cases, such a change may allow the deceased to still cast a glance to the "dimensionality of their past lives"; since, compared to the butterfly, they are spiritually far higher developed and are capable of self-reflection. To their surviving relatives, however, such glimpses must remain impossible because they have no notion of this new dimension. They are also unable to perceive them since they are confined to sensory perceptions.

2) In a completely different way, smallest pathogenic germs are invisible and yet always really existent. 150 years ago, people had no knowledge of them. Nobody knew why some people were taken ill with bubonic plague or smallpox, tuberculosis or diphtheria, splenic fever or tetanus.

Thus, during the 17th and 18th centuries most people still feared water, since they held water accountable for serious illnesses. That is why the use of perfume and powder increased dramatically.

Today, out of the blue, we have the "Corona" virus. The entire world suddenly goes haywire – unfortunately not always for medically sound reasons.

16

You could almost get the impression that a new war has broken out. Even borders are being closed. The actionist behaviours of some politicians results in unnecessary curfews and a ban on public gatherings. Panic purchases escalate, the shelves in the supermarkets are sometimes empty. The enemy is invisible.

Nobody can see these viruses, but everyone is afraid of them.

It is obvious, of course, that for some people they can lead to very severe medical conditions. However, this applies only to a small percentage of the population and especially old people, and those with severe pre-consisting conditions may even die. Many people are in a state of panic now, which is unfortunately further fuelled and often unreasonably exaggerated by some leading media. The pathogen eludes almost all forms of sensory perception and can only be detected biochemically. The fact remains that beings exist which suddenly cause most serious problems in the entire world. Basically, however, they are nothing but a "breath of nothing".

By the way, from a strictly physical point of view, we are also exactly that.

I will come back to this later.

3) It is only 150 years ago that "visible light" was only known as "physical radiation". Nevertheless, some contemporaries then considered the research in physical science to be "complete and finished". For this very reason, in 1874 the physicist *Philipp von Jolly (1809-1884)* strongly advised his student *Max Planck (1858-1947),* who became very famous later, not to study physics. Everyone knows today that Max Planck even became the founder of a completely new and unimaginably important field in physical science, that of "quantum physics", and that he was awarded the Nobel Prize for this.

If we examine the radiation spectrum known today, we notice that it is vast and that the "visible light" between 400 and 800 nm only takes up a miniscule part of it. Beyond the spectrum of "blue light" there are, for example, UV radiation, such as that of the Sun, all X-rays as well as gamma and cosmic radiation. Beyond the spectrum of "red light" there are, for example, infrared radiation, all radio waves, television waves and the alternating currents. They are all *really existent.*

And even if there were no radio or television sets (they were unknown to us in the past), these rays would still exist. Even today we cannot claim to know the full extent of the physical radiation spectrum.

Indeed, if we are unable to perceive some things with our senses this certainly does not mean they cannot *really* exist.

Our senses have always been so synchronised with each other that they only perceive things which are necessary for our everyday life and for our survival.

It was never necessary to develop "receiving devices", i.e. appropriately adapted senses, for radio waves or X-rays.

Therefore, could it not be that there are still unknown dimensions and spectra which have yet to be discovered?

Perhaps there is a world – or even worlds – which even physics can neither "grasp" nor "comprehend", but which nevertheless exists (exist) in a very real way and which has always especially nourished "physical science" like nothing else and has even enabled its development.

Mysterious Mathematics

Humans have always searched for universally valid rules to describe the world. In the course of thousands of years they have also recognised that in particular mathematics can help them to achieve this. It describes the world more precisely and predictably than any other science. Of course, this immediately raises the question as to whether mathematics might not be the actual basis of this world or, in other words, whether mathematics is really existent in our world and thus provides the ideal "red thread" for understanding the world.

This is exactly what I have long been convinced of.

The Greek philosopher and universal scholar of Late Antiquity *Proclus (412-485)* developed the theory of *emanation.*

18

According to this theory, the entire diversity of the world gradually builds up from a comprehensive but initially undifferentiated unity, which is regarded as the origin of everything. Proclus saw numbers as the key to comprehending nature and the cosmic soul. He therewith strongly influenced the German natural philosopher *Johannes Kepler (1571-1630)* towards the end of the Middle Ages. Keppler considered the number "3" as the most perfect number[6] of the "Divine Creation", for others it was the number "4".

All algorithms of computer systems are based on mathematics. Remote controls, mobile phones, GPS navigation systems and many more communicate with each other or with other devices by means of invisible electromagnetic waves.

The US physicist *Eugene Paul Wigner (1902-1995)* discovered fundamental principles of symmetry in elementary physics, for which he was awarded the Nobel Prize for Physics in 1963. He once said: *"The enormous usefulness of mathematics in the natural sciences is something bordering on the mysterious and there is no rational explanation of it."*

The Israeli astrophysicist *Mario Livio* is fascinated by the profound connection between mathematics and the physical world.

He draws attention, for example, to the proliferation of *Fibonacci numbers* in all areas of nature. This term goes back to the Italian mathematician *Leonardo da Pisa (1170-1240),* known as Fibonacci. He developed a simple sequence of numbers which he discovered by means of an intellectual game in which two rabbits and their offspring continuously reproduce in the same way every month. The result is the sequence 1,1,2,3,5,8,13,21,34 and so on. If you add up the respective last two numbers, you get the next number. If you divide the last but

---

[6] Not to be confused with a "perfect number" in mathematics which is the sum total of all its (positive) divisors. Example: 6 has the divisors 1, 2 and 3 (and of course 6). The sum of which is 6. Then the next perfect number is 28, since it has the divisors 1, 2, 4, 7 and 14, the sum of which is 28, etc.

one number by the last number, you get increasingly closer to the infinite sequence of numbers of the "golden section" (6-1-8). Practically everything in our world that proves to be optimal is characterised by the "golden section" and thus by the "Fibonacci Numbers".

For example, the coils in a snail shell are arranged according to the golden section as are the spiral coils of a hurricane over the Caribbean or the spiral arms of our Milky Way.

In 2020, the Berlin mathematician and President of the Berlin Free University *Professor Dr. Günter Ziegler* commented in a TV programme[7] on the many patterns on which apparently all phenomena in the physical world are based. He said: *"This phenomenon of repeatedly occurring shapes in minor and major matters and everywhere throughout the entire nature is not yet explained."*

There is mathematics in music as well:

The ancient Greeks already knew that harmonious sounding music follows simple mathematical ratios:

By measuring the distances on the strings of the musical instruments of those days, *Pythagoras (570-510 B.C.)* established that the three harmonic musical intervals, today known as octave, fifth and quart, are mathematically interrelated across the first four ordinal numbers: Any two notes an octave apart have a frequency ratio of 2:1, for a fifth the ratio is 3:2 and for a fourth the ratio is 4:3.

Johannes Kepler (1571-1630) recognised that there is also a "golden fifth" in which the frequency ratio is not 3:2, this means not 1.5 as in a normal fifth, but 1.618..... This corresponds to the "golden ratio", the measurement for the best or the most beautiful in our world.

Kepler also established that the orbits of all the planets around our Sun follow harmonious relationships. For him, the coordination of these harmonious relationships among the planets of our solar system is so distinct that they support each other *"as if they were parts of the same single structure"*.

---

[7] „Die Magie der Mathematik" (The Magic of Mathematics), German TV, 3SAT (2020)

Ultimately, when the extremely rare constellation occurs that all six (inner) planets are aligned, the total harmony of celestial movements resound as a perpetual polyphonic music, which ultimately remains inaudible since the planets in the sky have neither voice nor sound.[8]

Many other physical phenomena also follow the very simple relationship of two ordinal numbers: Among others, there is, for example, the ratio of hydrogen (H) to oxygen (O) in water (H_2O), which is 2:1. The relationship of the Moon's orbit around the Earth to its own rotation is 1:1, while one orbit round the Earth takes 27.3 days. In relation to the Earth, the Sun also rotates once round itself in 27.3 days; there are many other examples.

We then come to another sequence of numbers which also seems to be of great importance in our world and which ultimately is also only based on a simple geometric relationship
I will come back to this shortly.

Another example of physical phenomena in integer ratios: In our solar system, Mercury revolves around itself three times while orbiting the Sun twice. This shows that mathematics very precisely describes the physical laws of the universe, such as gravity or the speed of light (c). Since this happens in such a precise and comprehensive way, it is reasonable to assume that mathematics not only describes the world in an excellent way but that it is also a *really existent and fundamental part* of it. You will find a more detailed description of mathematical reflections in the second part of this book.

In numerous books since 1999, I have repeatedly postulated, described and explained universal phenomena which follow mathematical rules and laws.

With the aid of 3 "immaterial information points", which act just like three coordinates in a coordinate system, the smallest "finite" point, that is the smallest "physical" geometric figure, i.e. a circle, however small, can be exactly determined (see fig 2).

---

[8] Bialas, V., „Johannes Kepler", published by Verlag Beck (2004)

In accordance with the biblical doctrine *"grow and multiply"* only two further steps of "multiplication", based on pure logic, result in multiple new aspects:
Three finite circles are created, whereby the second circle opens up the first dimension (line) and the third – equally large – circle opens up the second dimension (area) by connecting their centres. The resulting intersections and contact points produce further simple geometric figures such as an equilateral triangle and a rectangular triangle.

With the aid of these, and again based on pure logic, the "growth" of the initial circle can be started.
At the same time the "Golden Section Φ" with the (infinite) number sequence <u>618</u>....is developed.

If we conclude this simple intellectual game in the second dimension, i.e. in the plane, then, by connecting the centre points of the formerly created "four initial circles", we arrive at a geometric figure on a completely new level of perfection: A square with four equal sides is created.

Out of a perfect *"unity"*, which is defined by purely "informational" ("spiritual") coordinates and is a "finite point", equivalent to a very small circle, an entirely new perfection in *"multiplicity"*, the square, is created.
While the circle still contains "infinity", since plane and circumference can only be determined by means of the irrational (infinite) number π (=Pi), the square only contains *"finitudes"*.

The ratio of the area of this square to its circumference, as the newly achieved perfection in "multiplicity", and its initial circle as the starting point in the perfect "unity", results in the (infinite) number sequence <u>273</u>......[9], which I termed, as early as 1999, "the limit of feasibility Ω".

---

[9] Explanation of the Greek symbols used here: π= Pi, Φ= Phi, Ω= Omega

Since in both cases (Φ und Ω) geometrical ratios are defined, the calculation system used for their "numerical representation" is, of course, completely irrelevant (Fig. 2).

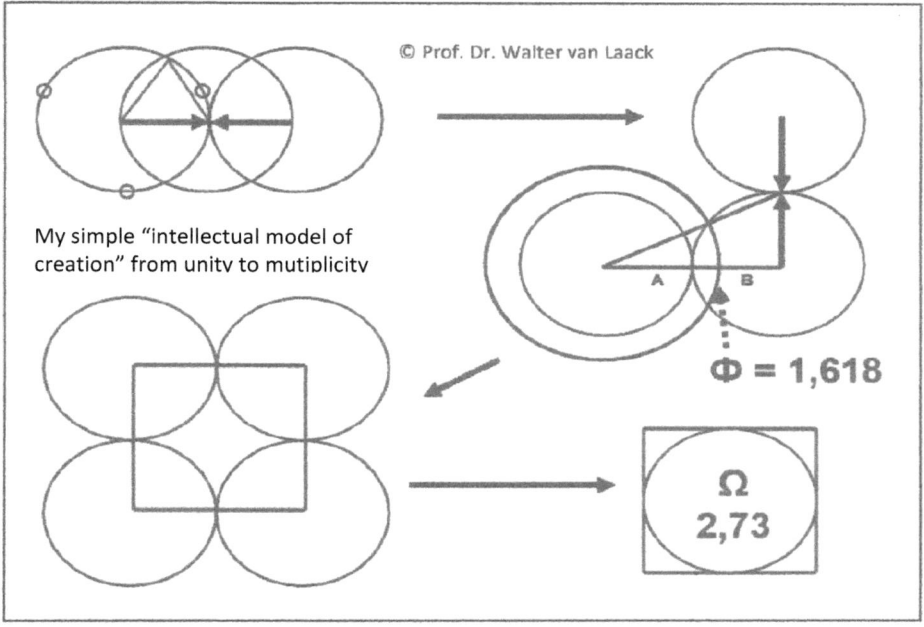

Fig. 2: See explanations above and further clarification in Part 2:
Two number sequences Φ und Ω, which significantly determine the universe, develop on the basis of a very simple mathematical intellectual game.

Another irrational, i.e. infinite, number which is immensely important in our world, which I already mentioned earlier, is the number π with its well-known sequence 3.14....

Pi (π) describes the geometric ratio of a circle's circumference to its diameter. Since here a relationship also exists between a round object, the circle, and a straight object, the circle's diameter, π is found, quite unexpectedly, everywhere in the world, for example when viewing the course of a river: The relationship between the actual length of a possibly extensively twisting river and the distance between its source and its mouth is approximately π. Every description of waves contains π, for light waves as well as for sound waves.

23

Simply everything with a round shape or everything growing spherically in our three-dimensional space, such as living cells, or everything expanding spherically, such as exploding stars, contains the infinite number sequence π = 3.14...

Peculiar Natural Constants

Meanwhile, a number of so-called natural constants are known now.
These are physically measurable quantities which are of crucial importance for the existence of our universe. Even though we can measure them experimentally, at least to some degree, i.e. "they remain blurred", it is still completely unknown what lies behind them, what connects them and why they are how they are and not different.
However, if they were not as stable – i.e. constant – as they obviously are, our universe would not exist. There would be neither atoms nor any kind of "solid matter", i.e. there would be no galaxies, planets or planetary systems – and, of course, no living beings.

In earlier books[10] I have already illustrated that, by means of the first four ordinal numbers alone, i.e. the numbers 1, 2, 3 and 4 plus two infinite number sequences 618... for the "optimum", i.e. the number sequence of the "Golden Section Φ", and 273... for the "limit of feasibility Ω", it is possible to define *all* currently known natural constants as number ratios (fractions) showing only very slight deviations from the measurements:

1) One important natural constant is the speed of light, denoted c.
Albert Einstein (1879-1955) recognised this as the absolute limit for any movement of physical bodies in a vacuum. It is defined as 2.99792458 x 10^8 m/s, i.e. almost 300,000 kilometres per second.

---

[10] e.g. described in detail in "To Perceive The World With Logic"(English edition 2008), and in other books published since 1999.

Presumably, however, the *ordinal number "3"* stands "behind" this measured value and is thus the really crucial and indicative measurement[11].

If you multiply the number 3 in the decimal system by any multiple of 10 (i.e. 3×10^n), then this amounts to the relevant *upper limit of the measured value of c.* The number 10 again is the sum of the first four ordinal numbers (=1+2+3+4).

Thus, the "ideal", on which the speed of light is possibly based, is defined by the decimal multiple of an "information, depicted by the *ordinal number 3*".

This *"informational ideal"* defines the speed of light, therefore, as a constant. The deviation of the actual measurement (2,9979...) from the number 3 is only 0.069%.

Light is *not* created by the interaction of *two bodies*, but emanates from only *one* body. Its value is directly related to the *expansion of space* in the universe. The product of *3×10^n* can stand for this. I have already explained this in detail in my earlier books.

In contrast, *effects between two interdependent (finite) bodies* in space are defined by the *reciprocal value of this product*. Then, instead of 3×10^n the following applies: $1 : (3 \times 10^n)$ or $1/3 \times 10^{-n}$ (cf. gravitation, for example).

2) The gravitational force (also termed gravity or force of attraction) is an effect *between two* three-dimensional, that means *finite,* i.e. physical or tangible, *bodies,* for example between the Earth and the Sun.

It follows, therefore, that the product of the number 2 (since there are two bodies) and the previously mentioned *reciprocal value* can be established here.

---

[11] This was described by the German chemist and natural scientist *Peter Plichta* in his book series "Das Primzahlkreuz" (The Prime Number Cross), published in the 1990s, which I gratefully took up, explained and reinforced with new references and analogies in earlier books.

Therefore it follows:

$2 \times (1/3 \times 10^{-n})$ or $2/3 \times 10^{-n}$. That is also $6.6666... \times 10^{-n}$.

The most important constant in our universe, apart from the speed of light, is the <u>gravitational constant (G).</u>

It was measured as $G = 6.67259 \times 10^{-19}$ (Nm^2/kg^2). This corresponds to the calculated value, if rounded up, with a deviation of only 0.088%.

3) The so-called <u>Planck effect quantum</u> or <u>Planck constant (h)</u> has a very similar factor.

It describes the *smallest effect* between *two bodies* in the universe. Therefore, the same reciprocal value ($1/3 \times 10^{-n}$) must again play a role here, since, as the reciprocal value of the factor for the expansion of space and the speed of light, it stands for all effects directed inwards.

Therefore, it must also be multiplied by <u>2</u> (i.e. <u>$2/3 \times 10^{-n}$</u>) since it is again a *measured effect between two bodies*.

In fact, the value is measured as h= 6.626075×10^{-34} (J/s). [12]

The deviation here is only 0.61% from the calculated value

4) The two most important atomic particles "proton" and "electron" are to be understood as being polar, i.e. in opposition to each other.

The proton is termed positively charged, the electron thus negatively charged. The hydrogen atom (H), by far the most important and the most widely spread atom in the entire universe, consists of only these two atomic particles, proton and electron.

Not only with respect to their opposite charges, but also with respect to their difference in size, they surely represent *two extreme opposites* within one atom.

This is particularly reflected in the ratio of their masses to each other. This is termed the <u>mass quotient</u>: It is also a natural constant and amounts to 1836.152701.

---

[12] J = Joule is also a decimal unit for energy. It is $1J = 1Nm$ (Newton metre) = 10 kgm^2/s^2

Isn't it amazing that here once again the previously mentioned factor $2/3 \times 10^n$ (whereby n=1), now multiplied by my key number for the "limit of feasibility Ω", i.e. 273..., arrives approximately at the same result?

It follows: $2/3 \times 10^1 \times 273... = 1820{,}9$.

The deviation is only just 0.84% from the calculated value.

5) Another very important natural constant is the <u>elementary charge</u>.

It should surely be an *optimal* quantity.

Here, as I have demonstrated, the mathematical blueprint of our world, which I have repeatedly postulated, provides an apt measurement, the "Golden Section Φ", with the number sequence 618..., i.e. defining the ratio of the so-called "continuous division" of 1.618 to 1.

The actually measured value of the <u>elementary charge</u> is 1,60217733 x 10^{-19} (C) /[13]. The deviation is only 0.99%.

6) Finally, a few words concerning the so-called <u>fine-structure constant</u> α, which determines the minimum distances on an atomic level – thus again limits – between two *smallest physical components.*

If it had a value other than 1 : 137.0359895 ($\pm$ something!), then atoms could not connect in the usual way to form molecules. Instead of water, metals, stones or sand, for example, we would only see a pulp of atoms.

Therefore, it should also have something to do with the number sequence for the "limit of feasibility Ω", i.e. the sequence 273...

Once again, we are dealing here with an *effect between two bodies* so that we should, analogous to the other constants, logically apply the factor 2 : 273 again (yet again a *reciprocal value*).

If we reduce this fraction we arrive at the value 1 : 136.5, which deviates only 0.39% from the actually measured value.

---

[13] C = coulomb = A-s = ampere-second: a decimal measurement for electrical charge

7) In spite of their not being "classical" natural constants in the recognised sense, there are indeed constants such as the number sequences Φ = <u>618</u>... and Ω = <u>273</u>... which obviously are misunderstood only too often, and which stand for "everything optimal" and the "limit of feasibility".

Modern science up till now only credits physical (sensual) perception with a *real existence*.

If we look upon the world within a framework based on elementary mathematical logic, then we notice that a multitude of observations demonstrates that the number sequence Ω = <u>273</u>... always marks limits while the number sequence Φ = <u>618</u>...repeatedly proves to be a measure for the optimum in the world and thus also for perfection.

At this point, I would like to return briefly to a very beautiful analogy. I was the first to develop it and referred to it in numerous earlier books – already in the past century – and I repeatedly pointed out in detail its proximity to reality:

First of all, it metaphorically explains the *emergence of "spirit" and (thereafter and thereof) of "matter"* out of the divine which is probably at the basis of everything and which will remain entirely indescribable for us:

From the "imaginary (or complex) number i"[14], which must be a real existing number, but cannot be arithmetically determined as the square root of "-1", we arrive at "+1" by squaring "-1", which we then square again and arrive at $(+1)^2$. Everything that exists and is generated in our world is based on this framework:

From a "divine entity" emerges the "informational" or "spiritual" and from this again the "physical" or "matter".

Everything physical in the world is subject to physical processes, for example, processes of regular cyclical growth and disintegration. These are also defined by a constant, the number known as <u>Euler's number (e = 2,72...)</u>. In mathematics it is the basis of the natural logarithm. It also

---

[14] Concerning "i", imaginary or complex numbers please refer to the second part of this book

28

describes the decrease in prime numbers with the increase of ordinal numbers ("distance from 1").

Once again, elementary mathematical number ratios seem to be the clearly determining factors for important physical inter-relationships. It seems that mathematics, especially geometry, and not physics is the basis for so many things in our universe. Arithmetic systems and calculation rules in comparison are man-made. They are reliable if they are based on and built on geometric standards.

There are obviously two limits for a physical existence, a "lower" one, derived from the infinite number sequence e = 27$\underline{2}$..., and a "higher" one, derived from Ω = 27$\underline{3}$.... The "limit of feasibility Ω" = $\underline{273}$... originates, as I have shown, *from the geometrical ratio of a new square to its starting circle (= 1,$\underline{273}$...).* This also allowed the "Golden Section" Φ = 1,$\underline{618}$... to be generated. It determines what is created in the world and how it is ideally formed. Since everything in our world is *dynamic,* we must also square the number sequence for the optimum Φ again and thus obtain $\underline{2,62}$...

The number sequence Ω = $\underline{273}$..., which I termed the "limit of feasibility Ω", can be determined by the first four ordinal numbers alone. The following applies: $1 + 2 + 3 + 4 = 10$ and $1^2 \times 3^4 = 81$.

This results in: $(10 + 81) \times 3 = 273$. Why this makes sense and is not just playing around with numbers (or even just a fiddle-faddle with numbers?), I will explain in detail and enhance in Part 2 of this book.

So we have four infinite number sequences, on which our world is based, whereby three differ by the factor "1". The "Golden Section Φ" stands for everything optimal, Euler's number represents all important physical processes such as generation and disintegration. Omega (Ω) as the "limit of feasibility" is self-explanatory. Since the limit of feasibility Ω results from the geometric ratio of a *new perfection* (square) to the *initial perfection* (circle) (via planes and circumferences, for spheres also via the volumes, see Fig. 2 and the context, it (Ω) also contains the fourth infinite number sequence, the constant π (Pi):

The following applies: 4 divided by 1,273... results in 3,141... = π.

About Coincidence, Chaos and Order

However, some natural physical forms and conditions cannot be determined by classical mathematics.

The French-American mathematician *Benoit Mandelbrot (1924-2010)* introduced a completely new geometry with infinitely recurring calculation cycles termed *iterations.*

If we visualise them, we can soon recognise regularities which Mandelbrot termed "fractals". Thereby a deep organisation throughout nature became apparent, the ever recurring "self-similarity". Mandelbrot described these regularities with number matrices so that fractals proved to be parts of the blueprints of our nature. Most of these self-similarities are not especially strict, for example, the leaves of a fern or vegetables. However, they are statistically significant, e.g. for coastlines or for blood vessels and nerve tracts in living bodies or for stars in galaxies.

A strict self-similarity is depicted by the following examples: Everyone knows Galton's nail board (Fig. 3). At the very top it starts with only one nail.

On each row below there is one nail more and the nails are arranged in a staggered order.

If we now drop a marble from above on the first nail it slips past all these nails and drops *randomly* into a box below.

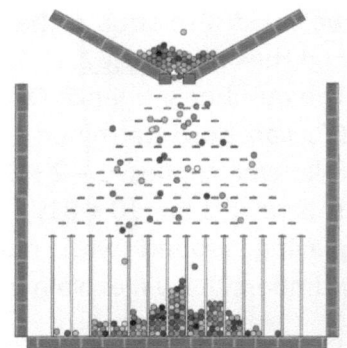

Fig. 3: Galton's nail board

If we now let 1,000 marbles roll down instead of just one, then we will soon notice that the marbles in the box below are arranged in a classical order: This is called the "Gaussian normal distribution", in reference to the German mathematician *Carl Friedrich Gauß (1777-1855).*

The resulting bell-shaped curve can also be developed by an arithmetical "binominal expansion" as propounded by the French mathematician and physicist *Blaise Pascal (1623-1662)*: We all know it from our school days, of course (Fig. 4).

First we calculate $(a+b)^2$ which results in **1a^2 + 2ab + 1b^2**.

Then we calculate $(a+b)^3$ which results in **1a^3 + 3a^{2}b + 3ab^2 + 1b^3**.

Then we calculate $(a+b)^4$ which results in **1a^4 + 4a^{3}b + 6a^{2}b^2 + 4ab^3 + 1b^4**.

And so on and so on.....

```
              1
            1  1
           1  2  1
          1  3  3  1
         1  4  6  4  1
       1  5 10 10  5  1
      1  6 15 20 15  6  1
    1  7 21 35 35 21  7  1
   1  8  28 56 70  56 28 8  1
   u. s. w.
```

Fig. 4: binominal expansion

Only the factors of the formula development are shown in Fig. 4, e.g. 1-1, next row 1-2-1, then 1-3-3-1, then 1-4-6-4-1, and so on.
It is easy to recognise that the numbers in one line are in each case the sums of the two numbers above to left and right.
If we now follow this process for long enough and then draw a curve according to these numbers, then this curve would correspond, with an ever smaller deviation, to the bell curve of the Gaussian normal distribution which we achieved, for example, by experimenting with Galton's nail board.

We could now draw an equilateral triangle into this curve with successive rows of hexagonal shapes just like honeycombs.
If we now mark all odd numbers in the rows black and all even numbers white, we arrive at the pattern pictured in Fig. 5 after only a few steps.

Fig. 5: Odd numbers in black, even numbers in white

If we proceed further in the same way, then, after many more calculatory steps, we will finally notice that the same patterns we saw on a small scale are regularly repeated on a large scale. The result is the pattern to the right, known as the Sierpinsky triangle (Fig 6), in reference to the Polish mathematician *Waclaw Sierpinski (1882-1969).*

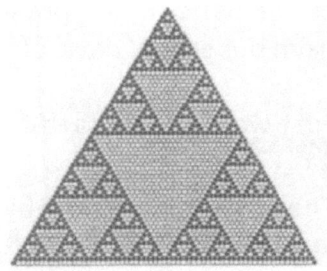

Fig. 6: Sierpinsky triangle

Initially this may sound like pure mathematics.
So you probably ask yourselves: where is the "golden bridge" to physical reality? Here an additional intellectual game.

It goes back to the German natural philosopher *Peter Plichta*[11]. I already drew attention to this in my very first book in 1999./[15] (Fig 7.)
Imagine an *equilateral triangle* with the apexes 1, 2 and 3.
Outside the triangle is a minute ball, e.g. a single gas atom.

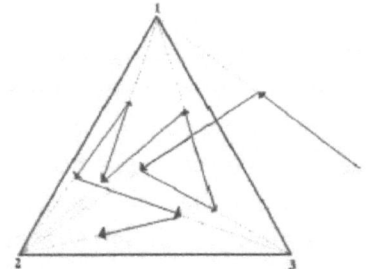

Fig. 7: Intellectual game according to *Plichta*

A random generator, which can only generate the numbers 1, 2 or 3, determines the first apex to which the ball should fly (here: apex 1).

We now draw a line from the sphere on the outside (the atom) to the determined corner of the triangle. Half way there the ball is stopped and the random generator determines a new apex to target (here: apex 2).

---

[15] "Plädoyer für ein Leben nach dem Tod und eine etwas andere Sicht der Welt" (engl.: „Pleading for life after death and a somewhat different view of our world", published only in German, 1999)

We draw a line to apex 2. Then the sphere is stopped again halfway, of course, and the random generator redirects it to yet another apex (here: apex 3).

This game continues perhaps for another 1.000 or 10.000 times at least. Once the ball is put into the triangle it cannot escape but keeps flying from one apex to the next randomly determined one. If we then, by means of a computer, delete all the connecting lines and only mark the stopping points, then this results again in a triangle with regular internal relationships, i.e. with a fractal pattern, although everything was determined by mere chance.

Again and again beautiful patterns appear due to an absolute order being established when a sufficient number of purely coincidental effects is achieved and then depicted. In the entire universe, all coincidences in physics finally lead to order again, and this means order on a new and higher level.

The experiment (the game) and the mathematical calculation once again lead to *the same* results. In the long run, therefore, all initially chaotic conditions result in a fascinatingly beautiful order.

In reverse conclusion we can justifiably assume that once again we can aptly describe the world with mathematical logic or, as *Galileo Galilei (1564-1642)* once expressed it in a more extensive way: *"The universe is written in the language of mathematics."*

Meanwhile, we know, by means of experimental studies, that elementary mathematics is already inherent in plants and lower animals and it is obviously embodied in every kind of brain, at least in a rudimentary form.

This applies to the carnivorous Venus flytrap as well as to insects and fish. Of course, it also applies to many birds and to mammals up to and including monkeys. It has been proven that they are all able to count and their understanding of quantities grows depending on the level of their development. They are also able to distinguish between all elementary geometric shapes. A few years ago, for example, it was established that fish can effortlessly discriminate between circles, triangles and squares.

Even babies, only a few months old, are able to do this without having learned it. And their mathematical understanding is initially quite similar to that of monkeys.

Matter is Really an Illusion

Mathematics also seems to be the determining common ground for the development of the universe and all important cornerstones of coexistence. No other system seems adequate to offer a suitable alternative. It seems that elementary mathematics is almost certainly not a human invention, even if humans working with it ultimately started to add some inventions and expand on it in order to render it better usable for their purpose and thus simplify their lives.

Elementary mathematics seems to *"really exist"* in this world. If there were no humans, the universe would still very much exist, since mathematics facilitates its existence and effectively influences and structures it everywhere.

However, what is elementary mathematics? It is the most "prosaic" and thus most "objective" basis for information, without any "subjectivity". It establishes the universal set of rules. It determines the framework of our world objectively and unambiguously. It is the core and the essence of everything "informational" in this world. *It exists before anything else exists.* It is the basis of physics and thus the origin and the basis of the physical world which emerges and develops with it and which is moulded in accordance with its rules. It is also "logos" which was translated from the *Gospel of John* as "word": *"In the beginning was 'logos' and 'logos' was with God and God was 'logos'".*

However, we humans live in this physical world and we only know this. Mathematics is considered by many to be a useful aid, but ultimately a mere human invention. In human conception, any kind of information requires a physical medium known to us, e.g. our brain, which is,

34

therefore, considered by many to be the creator of spirit and consciousness. When the brain dies it means, that the spirit, allegedly produced by it, must also cease to exist.

Those who think like this even believe this to be a sign of enlightenment – no matter how naïve it all may sound in the context of what is said here and with regard to the many images, metaphors and analogies of great naturalists, scientists and philosophers.

The Greek philosopher *Plato (428-348 B.C.)* already tried to correct this notion with his famous allegory of the cave. At the beginning of his book *Politeia* his teacher *Socrates (469-399 B.C.)* tells the story: People are imprisoned and chained in a cave for their entire life. They are forced to gaze at the wall in front of them and cannot even turn their heads to look behind them where there is an exit.

They cannot even see their fellow prisoners, just the wall of the cave in front of them. There is a fire in a shaft behind them which provides some light for them. They cannot see the fire either, only the shadows on the cave wall in front of them.

People are walking back and forth between their backs and the fire. They are carrying objects and come and go through the exit.

However, the prisoners can see nothing of what is happening behind them. They are only able to see the shadows cast upon the cave wall in front of them which are caused by the activities behind them. Even when the people behind them speak, they cannot relate these sounds to people since they know nothing of their existence. Sounds of the people talking or singing just echo off the walls. So, the prisoners must assume that the shadows are singing and talking. Only what is happening on the wall or what is echoed by the walls is the entire reality for the prisoners as long as they live.

Let us assume now that the prisoners are enabled to engage in a scientific study of their (pseudo) reality: They would then develop a science of shadows, and by means of their science, they would search for regularities and then deduce predictions from them. The narrator in Plato's allegory, i.e. Socrates, now asks his dialogue partner *Glaucon* to imagine what would happen if one of the prisoners were released, brought out to the sunlight and he would be confronted with *true reality.*

This person would be painfully blinded by the light and would consider the entirely new scenery now unfolding in front of him as utterly surreal.

Only the reality of the shadows on the cave wall, which he had experienced, would be his reality. If we were to assure him that this was not the case, that only the new reality was the real thing, he would, of course, not believe it; to him it would be a completely absurd idea.

This beautiful famous cave allegory by *Plato* reflects exactly what it is that makes so many people today walk through life with blinkers on: They do not recognise reality and they simply cannot imagine it, in spite of so many coherent and very plausible indications. They turn a blind eye to reality because their research is often utterly monomaniacal and constrained within narrow limits and, accordingly, their life and their ability to think is also usually limited.

However, just a small intellectual leap forward could liberate them and could at least make them accept the hypothetical assumption that "information" is really existent. Information would not need a "physical carrier substance", at least not in the way we imagine it, as we can only have certain images and ideas of such "physical carriers".

All information is based on elementary mathematics and is determined by basic mathematical conditions. (Information) clusters, i.e. larger coherent information groups, emerge in the course of immense periods of time all of which are to be found within the framework of an even more comprehensive evolution of information – or, generally speaking, of the "informational". There are also additional attributes inherent in the informational which then gradually unfold: *life and spirit.*

But that is not all: On closer inspection, the question soon arises as to whether the physical or material world is actually real, this world which most of us already assume to be at least the dominant one anyway, but

36

which is often also assumed to be the only existing reality. Or is it perhaps only the product of a spiritual, i.e. generally speaking again, an "informational world", on which it is actually based?

So, how real is this physical world really?

Quantum physics, still relatively young, has exposed everything which was previously considered "physically orthodox", as being questionable and "fuzzy". Crucial interpretations of resulting phenomena should be scrutinised again. Admittedly, most physicists today accept them as a given. But how many of them have really ever understood this?

This includes, for example, the interpretation of light being both particles *(photons)* and waves simultaneously, since, based on our current world view, the famous *double-slit experiment* actually makes this interpretation irrefutable.

This also includes the almost esoteric conclusion of some otherwise very naturalistic physicists that it is possible to sever the so-called *entanglement* of interconnected particles over any cosmic distance *(superposition)* by taking a "conscious decision" to "pick off" one of the two particles, thereby causing a *"collapse of the wave function".*

If you do not understand this right away, it does not matter, since it contradicts any everyday experience anyway. Therefore, there is no point in explaining it in more detail here. I would rather refer to my earlier books in which I explained this in detail. Please just simply accept here my conclusion: I think that all this is based on entirely wrong conceptions.

Please, do not misunderstand me: Of course, the behaviour of light displaying characteristics both of particles and waves simultaneously, as correctly observed in the double-slit experiment, is an absolutely *verifiable phenomenon.*

It is also true that, when we try to pick off one specific far-away *variant* of interconnected particles "at the other end", we only ever "pick off" the other one.

Once again, the phenomena are correctly observed: It is just the interpretation following the observation which seems absurd. The interpretations seem to be incorrect because the physicists, who engage in it, are sitting in Plato's cave and many of them are unwilling to recognise reality. Some of them are admittedly not even in a position to actually see it, since they lack the crucial prerequisites for doing this. These are, in turn, of an *informational* nature: They cannot "see" the wood for the trees. But in order to see the reality, a *paradigm shift in thinking* is essential.

I believe that it is absolutely impossible to develop an understanding for the true interrelationships if someone remains stuck in our conventional physics with the dogmatic assumption that matter is the basis of everything in this world and the essence of the entire universe.
This is why the German physicist *Hans-Peter Dürr (1929-2014)[16]*, whom I hold in high esteem, repeatedly called for the *"necessity to change paradigms"*. To illustrate this, Dürr said in one of his inspiring lectures, that we should image the world as a gateau consisting of different layers.
Dürr then elaborates: *"This gateau, it is the world. And now we must describe it: what is the world? It depends on whether I am a baker or someone who eats the gateau. A baker says, it is quite simple, a layered gateau consists of several layers of different materials, such as a layer of dough and another with nuts and then a layer of fruit and so on. But the person who eats the gateau says that is not true at all, because he cuts a slice out of the cake and says that this piece already has a structure. And now the two are arguing. Who is right? These are the disputes we (in science) have to face all the time. If these opponents would now just wait until they put the whole thing back together, then they would realise that they have the same gateau again. It depends on the motive behind it: what is considered to be there first, i.e. to be the basis, and what is the derivative. So, these are two different paradigms, both successful if taken to their logical conclusion. But there is a certain difficulty: Is it really true that, if we put everything back together again,*

---

[16] Professor Dürr and I were invited for a joint workshop on this subject in Kleve, Germany, in February 2014. Unfortunately, he was taken ill shortly before, he had to cancel by telephone and finally died on 18th May 2014, so that to my greatest regret this workshop had to be cancelled.

*we have the very same gateau? Not exactly true! When I take the
dough, it sticks together, the pieces of gateau, on the other hand, keep
falling apart. So, I must attach some sticky tape between the pieces for
the two results to resemble each other. Well, but if I now ask, whether
the new physics is merely a third way of cutting the gateau, the answer
is: No.*
<u>*"The answer is more or less: there is no gateau at all."*</u>

To put it bluntly, Dürr says nothing other than that matter, as we think
we know and feel it, is pure illusion.
Let us now consider an atom. For this we could choose any atom, but
the most omnipresent in the entire universe is the hydrogen atom. This
atom is particularly suited for illustrating the real key message of Hans-
Peter Dürr's statement.
Atoms have been known since the 5th century BC.[17]
Although we know today that atoms are not indivisible, they are, as
some kind of "particle arrangement", nevertheless the smallest building
blocks of matter. The hydrogen atom consists of only two such
"particles", one proton, which is also the atomic nucleus, and one
electron, which circles round this nucleus, the proton.
In the course of the last 100 years, this simple concept has long since
been improved and the following applies: In principle, these two
"particles" are a mere "breath of nothing". It is not possible, for
example, to localise the electron (to define its current location) and to
measure its momentum simultaneously. This applies to all
complementary properties referring to smallest particles (Heisenberg's
uncertainty principle).
However, such subtleties are irrelevant here for now.

For the sake of simplicity, let us stay with the model with the two
particles of the hydrogen atom, its proton and its electron. If we

---

[17] Atomos means "indivisible". The doctrine of indivisible smallest particles (atomism) goes back
to the Greek philosopher *Leukipp* and his scholar *Demokrit (d. approx. 370 BC.)*

imagine the proton to be about the size of a cherry, then the electron would be even smaller than a pinhead.

But the significant factor in this picture is that the electron would circle around the proton at a distance of about two kilometres. And between the proton and "its" electron there is *nothing, absolutely nothing, no matter at all*. Hans-Peter Dürr only spoke of "relationships" and his "physical grandfather", the German physicist *Werner Heisenberg (1901-1976)*, spoke of "effects".

It is a fact that every atom is basically a giant "empty sphere with no defined outer skin and without real matter between the particles inside". Everything just clings together somehow. Actually there are only forces. They are known as strong or weak nuclear forces. Somehow they exist and hold everything together, extremely accurately and *mathematically exact*. However, nobody knows what these forces – or *effects* or *relationships* – really are.

Every atom in the entire universe is basically a *"breath of nothing"*. These "mysterious forces" alone are holding everything together, and they determine what is formed from these atoms and what remains stable. Although they can be measured and exactly calculated, which means that they must really exist, they cannot be explained (substantially). They could only exist if we (finally) were to implement the paradigm shift postulated by Professor Hans-Peter Dürr. This would mean accepting information, or generally speaking everything "informational", in principle as being just as *really existent* as planets, suns, stones, plants or simply everything physical, such as, for example, human beings.

From a physical point of view, we all, you and I and all celestial bodies in the universe, are a mere *"breath of nothing"*.

The reason why we all only feel quite different – depending on the circumstances as hard or soft – in this "elusive realm between nothing and nothing" is, because, from a physical point of view, everything and we all are of exactly the same matter and because everything fits together perfectly like a key and its lock.

40

In addition, however, we could also quite easily imagine countless other partial worlds within this whole, completely incomprehensible world, at least from a purely mathematical point of view.

We are already speaking with certain restrictions when we mean the universe, because we only consider the physical side of it.

But there is probably so much more which we do not perceive, which we even cannot perceive. So we let ignorance shape our way of thinking. Of course, we can neither see nor somehow measure these possibly many " world elements" within this world since our sensory organs and their "extended physical counterparts", i.e. from microscopes to telescopes, are also made of the same matter as we ourselves. That is why we cannot perceive them. This sounds inconceivable; it is, however, nevertheless imaginable and plausibly supported by many indications. I call such imaginable "parallel worlds" simply *"phase-shifted"*.

So, with our physical methods, we are in no position to assess what else could exist outside the purely physical world, and, I am convinced, probably does exist.

We are, therefore, not in a position – and many of us unfortunately are not even willing – to understand that the essence of this world is probably *scarcely the part which we can perceive with our senses.*

Furthermore, there seems to be a much larger part, the unfathomably vast world of the "informational". This, however, is part of the _non_-physical component of the world, which seems to be the real basis of the universe.

And in addition, it controls absolutely crucial relationships with the utmost mathematical precision (see Part 2).

The "informational world" is also the stronger reality, in the same way as the "world of negative numbers" is the "stronger reality" in mathematics. It is stronger than that of the "positive numbers" at the end of a "chain of development", which starts from a "world of imaginary (complex) numbers" through the "world of negative numbers" to the "world of positive numbers" (see Part 2).

In order to comprehend the actual size of our world with any reasonable accuracy, we must go beyond physics, and we must learn to look beyond the boundaries of completely different, indeed all, subject areas. We must also learn to think "metaphysically".

It is for this purpose that we possess our intellect, or, as the famous German philosopher *Immanuel Kant (1724-1804)* expressed it in the 1780s, our *"reason"*. First of all, we must collect all the different phenomena, observations and measurements, then weigh them against each other and then, if possible, draw the most "reasonable" conclusions from them. This is how we gain new knowledge.
We cannot gain further knowledge either by religious convictions or by purely scientific conclusions alone.
Only "our reason" *(logos)* can achieve this, according to Immanuel Kant. Kant also recognised that we may indeed be endowed with "reason", which, however, could by no means be produced by our physical brain: Chemical mixtures in a factory do not produce a chemist either.

Kant, however, went one crucial step further, since he also recognised that our reason or our intellect is by no means something collective, i.e. *not some kind of "collective reason"*, unlike Carl Gustav Jung's[18] concept of the "collective unconscious" which must only be coaxed out but is basically inherent in everyone.
According to Kant, "reason" is a purely *"individual quality"*, more pronounced in some, less in others, but in every case it is a purely individual trait which can be learned to a certain extent. It is also based on an individual learning process. I will come back to this later.

And what conclusion do we now draw from all this?
Reason - and so our intellect – are important attributes of our "mental skills". They are "immaterial values".
They belong to the "informational part" of our world.

---

[18] Carl G. Jung (1875-1961), Swiss psychiatrist, founder of the analytical psychology

We humans (as well as all animals, depending on their level of individual development within the evolution of life, of course) have thus always belonged to both worlds which actually constitute our universe: We are part of the larger spiritual or "informational" reality or world, which ultimately always precedes everything physical. Simultaneously, of course, we are also part of the physical or material world, which emerges from it and is shaped by it, i.e. that part of the whole world which many erroneously claim to be the only really existing one.

I already mentioned it briefly above: The great philosophers of ancient China, such as Lao Tzu[19] and Confucius[20], already recognised the mutually supporting and complementing polar symmetrical dualism and to illustrate this they created the image with two opposing flames, Yin and Yang, where each also contains a part of the

Fig. 1: Yin and Yang

other (Fig. 1 and 8). The spiritual (or informational) world is *one* part of this whole world, the physical universe being the *other*. They are both in opposition to each other and they are mirror-images of each other: polar-symmetrical.

They support and complement each other. In principle, the physical part proceeds in *cyclical progressions*, whereas the immaterial, informational part proceeds in *linear progressions*. On the physical part, everything is *finite and limited,* whereas on the non-physical, the immaterial or informational part everything is *infinite and unlimited.* Both polar-symmetrical versions are always found on every level of development. Both versions are, in variable dominance, always part of the same coin.

---

[19] Lao-tzu, 6th century BC, Chinese philosopher
[20] Confucius, 551-479 BC, Chinese philosopher and social ethicist

Information and Matter are Polar-Symmetrical

The course of all matter in the universe is of *finite* nature and progresses cyclically: Celestial bodies of all kinds emerge and develop until they reach their zenith, where they may even remain on a more or less constant level for many billions of years. At some time or other, however, they all start to decline. Our Sun will also run out of fuel in a few billion years. It will then blow up to a huge ball of fire, a "red giant", within a relatively short time, and will swallow up the planets closest to it, probably also the Earth. After it has finally burnt out, it will collapse to a stellar corpse, a white dwarf.

Compared to other stars, our Sun is small and has only a low mass. Stars with very large masses will inflate into super-giants and eventually explode. This is known as a supernova. The nuclei of smaller stars are subject to extreme pressure which forces the electrons of the atoms into the protons. They then turn into neutrons, whereby so-called neutron stars are created which have small diameters and a very high angular momentum: this means they rotate at a very high speed. The nuclei of larger stars are subject to even higher pressure and they are compressed to such a degree that in the end only an extremely small piece of matter remains with extremely high density resulting in an extremely strong gravity (gravitation). This incredibly small something is (inaccurately) known as a "black hole".

Some physicists would certainly like to replace the word "extreme", which I used three times here, by the word "infinite".
However, infinity does not exist in physics.
This would, therefore, be wrong. In this respect, the term "hole" is also wrong, since it cannot be a hole. In fact, some kind of mass must remain which – although only minute – must be immensely condensed and, therefore, possess an extremely large force of gravity (gravitation).

All physical objects, without exception, follow similar cyclical courses of emergence or birth, growth up to their zenith or maximum, followed by their slower or faster degradation resulting in decay or death. This also applies to all living bodies, ours included. A well-known proverb expresses it so aptly: That is the course of all THINGS …

We humans are all conceived and are born after nine months. We grow up and reach our physical zenith in our young adulthood. We then remain apparently on a fairly stable level for a few years. In fact, however, we start going downhill physically very early on, at first we hardly notice it but later we register the increasing speed. In the end, death awaits all of us. But here again, this only reflects *one side of the coin.*

There is another side to the coin: The cornerstones of the other side must then relate polar-symmetrically to the first, the physical side of BEING and on every further level of existence.

This means, however, that what is *limited* (body) becomes *unlimited* (soul) and what was *finite* (our life in the "here and now") becomes *infinite (or unlimited) and eternal* from our point of view.

The *cyclical* development of everything physical in the "here and now" comes to an end with death. However, the development of the "informational-spiritual", which has progressed up to that point, has always progressed in a *linear* upwards pointing direction and it will, therefore, unabatedly continue to do so. (see also Part 2).

The Modern Zeitgeist Credo

For most of our contemporaries, especially those in the "western world" and in those countries where socialist ideas in the spirit of social thinking continue to prevail, not all of my explanations will be easy to digest. On the other hand, followers of some esoteric ideas are quick to agree, but often change their minds when I draw their attention also to the consequences which follow from there and which might not necessarily agree with their view of the world.

Religious people are sometimes so strongly dominated by the ideas of their religious communities and churches that, in the worst case, they consider my thoughts as sacrilege.

In short, it has certainly not always been easy for me with my statements given above to be heard as I have experienced repeatedly over the last twenty-five years.

Nonetheless, I believe I am on the right path.

Especially the current "Corona crisis", which in many respects has put the entire world under immense stress for over a year now and has kept many people in thrall, makes it evident to me that enlightenment and science and thus well-founded ideas of the world cannot be worth all that much.

In fact, even "enlightened" people and those supposedly devoted to "science", often seem to wear blinkers nowadays, with a tunnel vision firmly fixed, and they appear rather resistant to all kinds of facts.

Such facts usually show up in figures and data. They are then statistically analysed and depicted in curves and graphic images. This helps to render them easily interpretable, but this also presupposes that they are not selectively processed and manipulated in accordance with personal ideas and preconceived convictions, as is unfortunately often the case.

So, caution is the mother of wisdom and that refers absolutely to any kind of statistics. The former British Prime Minister *Winston Churchill (1874-1965)* is credited with the modified quote: *"Do not trust any statistics you have not falsified yourself."*

But even this does not seem to be true.[21]

Calculated and simultaneously very subtle manipulations of statistics are part of the daily routine of the governmental propaganda machinery and, unfortunately, also of main media which then publish them effectively. Currently we can frequently detect this in impressive quantities.

Hence, a large number of citizens are easily manipulated by those who have a vested interest in it and who know how to implement it properly for their own purpose. The Corona pandemic seems to be an example

---

[21] According to Werner Barke: "I only trust the statistics I have falsified myself" (2004)

for this and it leaves deliberately a rather unpleasant aftertaste, consistent with the title of this chapter. The title "The Modern Zeitgeist Credo" points out that even nowadays we are confronted almost daily with many ideas claiming to be confirmed knowledge which in fact they are not.[22]

I do not want to elaborate further on the cosmological background of our universe here and, with reference to my earlier books, I leave it to the reader to obtain more information on this topic. Only this much here: Accordingly, the universe as we (want to) know it today must have developed basically within an unimaginably short fraction of a second some 13.8 billion years ago *("inflationary phase")*. The origin of the whole in its entirety is assumed to have been a *"singularity"* in which *"quantum fluctuations"* could be imaginable since "nothing" does not exist.

Without going into further detail, however, I would like to remark the following:
Such ultrashort times of development in such unimaginably short fractions of a second can never be proven scientifically, of course, – no matter what it was and especially not 13.8 billion years after the event. Therefore, this must for ever remain pure speculation, simply based on computer simulations. However, this certainly makes it not at all better than many ideas of esotericism, which is the most intractable enemy for such scientists anyway.

A "singularity" does not make sense either, since it would mean *"infinity"* which does not exist in physics – and can thus not exist anywhere in the physical universe. It is physically correct though that there is no nothing, since thus we would basically be close to singularity again.

---

[22] Credo (lat.): "I believe", from credere = to believe. In the German language Credo also means the Confession of Faith

However, in mathematics we have indeed "nothing" which is described by *zero*. It is a "spiritual" or *"informational placeholder for nothing"* and simultaneously a mirror axis for the two worlds of numbers, the negative and the positive numbers, already mentioned above.

In practice, this "information" is omnipresent, and I suggest it to be considered as being *really existent*.

Since there are many conclusive indications for this assumption, it seems to me far less speculative than the otherwise presently supported ideas about the origin and existence of our universe which are always defined as "knowledge".

The so-called "quantum fluctuations" if decoded are probably nothing but the expression of a *"dynamic of information"*.

"Space", in the sense known to us, would not be needed before the alleged big bang scenario.

In a similar manner, we can here approach the crucial points as to what our universe needs according to today's prevailing view, in order to be able to exist at all in the way we actually observe it.

After all, there are "dark matter" and "dark energy".[23]

The phenomena on which such claims are based are quickly explained. The universe seemingly keeps expanding further and further. However, not the galaxies themselves are moving apart but entire clusters of galaxies are drifting apart at an increasingly faster rate. We could compare the universe to a sourdough dotted with raisins:

The clusters of galaxies are the single raisins. When the dough now rises and expands the raisins will drift further and further apart while being baked.

But it seems that there is no such thing as an end to the expansion of our universe, as was previously discussed. Quite the opposite is the case: The expansion even seems to increase in speed as scientists claim to know.

---

[23] For "discovering" "dark energy" the three scientists Saul Perlmutter, Brian Schmidt and Adam Riess were even awarded the Nobel Prize in Physics in 2011.

However, this is exceptionally puzzling, since technically the gravity of all masses (in this case: the raisins) should have the exact opposite effect and thus pull everything together again at some stage. The same applies to a ball thrown into the air, due to gravity (gravitation) it falls back to the ground.

Therefore, it seems that there must be another force which we can neither measure nor yet see.

Physicists refer to it as "dark energy".

It is supposed to be responsible for the increasingly faster expansion of the cosmos.

On the other hand, however, even the total visible mass of "all the clusters of raisins in the universe put together" is far too small to explain why, for example, galaxies do not fly apart although they are spinning as fast as they are.

After all, rotation creates another force known as centrifugal force, which works against the force of gravity.

We know this from centrifuges in which, for example, moulds filled with chocolate are spun around so that the chocolate covers the insides leaving a hollow form, such as a chocolate Easter bunny or a Santa Clause which are so popular with our children. From this, scientists conclude that there must be much more mass, which exerts gravity itself, in addition to the known visible matter. However, since we can neither measure nor even see it, we speak of "dark matter". Scientists today think that this is the only way of explaining the motion patterns and structures which can actually be observed.

We must now bear in mind that only 5% of the entire universe is visible matter. Another 20% is "dark matter" and 75% must be "dark energy", or to put it in casual and simple words: We know nothing at all about 95% of the entire universe. In fact, all we have are speculative ideas about it. Nevertheless, these ideas have long been portrayed as essential or, as we like to say today, "system-relevant" pillars of knowledge and thus the current modern view of the world is constructed based upon these ideas. In this way, almost everything could be plausibly explained today. Of course, "God" is no longer needed: More than 200 years ago the French mathematician *Pierre-*

Simon Laplace (1749-1827) expressed this in a similar way. When Napoleon asked him where God still had his place in such a scientific view of the world, he said: *"Sire, I do not need this hypothesis."* [24]

In the course of the last 200 years, a purely naturalistic (physical) view of the world has emerged. Since then, everything spiritual has been classified as a mere product of matter or, in a more philosophically sophisticated term, as an "epiphenomenon" of the physical world. This reduces spirit to a purely incidental side effect. What I think about this should be quite clear by now: I think this is pure nonsense.

The fact is, of course: In general, matter develops coincidentally and acts or interacts coincidentally as long as it is inanimate.
Coincidences happen, of course, as I explained earlier in the chapter "About Coincidence, Chaos and Order".
And yet, pure coincidences finally always result in order. Insofar, the development history of all "inanimate" objects, which seems so agonisingly long to us, is only logical and inevitable, since it does indeed take a very long time, often an exceptionally long time, before coincidence turns into order. This applies to everything physical in this world, including all defined, i.e. finite or three-dimensional structures.

Let us take a look at the development of our cosmic home, the planet Earth and let us accept the modern zeitgeist credo as maintained by modern science: According to this, the universe has existed for about 13.8 billion years. About 4.5 to 4.7 billion years ago the Sun emerged and relatively shortly afterwards, also the Earth. About one billion years later, the first sign of life appeared on the new Earth and for another three billion years the forms of life remained very simple and unsophisticated. Thereafter, however, the development gained speed: During the last mere 500 million years up until today, basically every

---

[24] In the original: The French astronomer Pierre Laplace (1749-1827) answered Napoleon's question where in his Mécanique céleste (celestial mechanics) God would have a place with: "Sire je n'avais pas besoin de cette hypothèse".

form of life existing today has developed and also everything that existed previously but was extinguished long ago.

The dinosaurs, for example, emerged about 250 million years ago and they died out completely about 60 million years ago. Although simple forms of mammals already existed in the late dinosaur age, their development really took off after the dinosaurs were extinguished. The first anthropoid apes developed 15 to 18 million years ago and the first humans more than one million years ago. So, humans also needed a very long period of time to become "civilised".

Stone Age man lived about 10.000 years ago. That spans only about 400 generations before today.[25]

It took immense periods of time in the beginning for life to emerge and develop. Very gradually at first, with an accelerating pace later, more complex and increasingly even more complicated forms of life developed – and, above all, they developed on a higher "spiritual level". But even between the "spiritual level" of Stone Age man and that of many of us humans today, a further and especially major leap forward in the development of mankind seems to have occurred.

But why does evolution need such immense time differences? Why did it take hundreds of millions of years for the physical body to develop from a single cell organism through all kinds of plant and animal forms to us humans? After all this time, humans today do not differ significantly in their physical appearance compared to their ancestors, the Stone Age people, who lived 10.000 years ago, i.e. 400 generations ago.

And there is hardly any difference in the anatomy of human brains between then and now: The human brain has hardly changed at all between Stone Age and modern times.

Nevertheless, a kind of quantum leap has taken place within this short period of time. And within this comparatively short period of time, the biggest leap has indisputably happened over the last 100 to 200 years.

---

[25] One generation takes about 25 years

If we take a closer look here, these leaps in humans seem to be of a purely spiritual or informational nature and they are not equally recognisable in everyone. In other words, while no significant physical (substantial) changes can be found, there are without doubt major differences noticeable solely on a spiritual or, as I like to term it, on a purely "informational level". While evolution still exists in humans it happens now to a growing degree between humans.

Even though in experiments simple "spiritual contents" can be sometimes demonstrated and provoked in physical "engrams", almost everything else we achieve *with* our brain in everyday life and beyond remains a mystery. Also, the performance of the brain has nothing whatsoever to do with its size. The brains of whales and elephants are larger than those of humans, but this does not make them intellectually superior. Even if a person only has half a brain this does not necessarily mean this person is handicapped compared to others, as many incidental findings have often shown – this applies at least when the reduction in brain mass is not brought about suddenly. Anatomical examinations of the brain and its parts also show that the nerve tracts simply run in the three directions of space.

Neither do we currently know what constitutes our "ego", how our "personality" develops and what it is. And where is "consciousness" located? There are simply no areas *in* the brain which are responsible for such aspects. We can always only say that an area is involved in a function.

Examples of Siamese twins joined at the head, for example, who share large areas of one and the same brain, and even those areas which are commonly assumed to be the "producers of the ego" indicate something else: These twins are always two personalities who think and feel in different ways.[26]

In fact, we know nothing at all about such "memory storage positions". With some justification we may assume that they are not even positioned *in* the brain.

---

[26] E.g. Lori and Reba (since 2007: George) Shappell, b. 1961, Pennsylvania (USA)

With all their diverse experiments, researchers have found so far nothing but extremely specialised areas which are *somehow involved* in individual processes which I only mention as examples here and I could name many more. Although these brain areas have something to do with the processes, they do not create the characteristics and abilities which become visible externally.

Some areas of our brain are certainly *also* involved in the production of important items, such as hormones in brain glands.
However, for the crucial spiritual matters the brain probably serves primarily as a complex device or even as an extensive equipment pool. Although the brain is the piano with its keyboard, it is by no means identical with the pianist playing it.
In 2004, ten renowned German brain researchers jointly signed a so-called *"German Brain Manifesto"*, probably in a kind of "high-spirit recklessness". According to this, brain research would be able, in the course of the next ten years, to expose and describe all the previously listed questions and processes and many more, as brain-manufactured processes.
A snowball's chance in hell! None of this has turned out to be true, and meanwhile it is many years after the date fixed by the manifesto.

When I was still active in my own practice and I operated a lot in my operating theatre, one of the theatre nurses came to me one morning rather exited and told me that her son's biology teacher had told them that *"love is merely a chemical reaction"*.
This statement afflicted him immensely and he told his mother at home.
My answer was that this teacher seemed to be "poor in spirit" and had obviously not understood much about the world yet.

Why is Evolution sometimes a Snail and sometimes a Sprinter?

Without doubt, there is an evolution of "(physical) things", such as galaxies, stars and planets, or mountains and rock formations, etc. The evolution of "non-living" things takes immense periods of time.
In contrast, however, there is also an "evolution of life" and of "animate things" or, as we term them, "living beings".
These are also physical bodies (things), however, they are, in addition, also alive, often they move around and they reproduce.
Even single-cell organisms are alive, stones are not. Plants are alive, mountains are not. Animals and humans are alive, planets and stars are not.
The aforementioned physical but "non-living" things may offer a multitude of preconditions which may be indispensable for "life" on their own or in combination with others; however, they are not alive.

If we now compare the evolution of "physical *and* living" things with that of physical but *"non-living"* things we recognise immediately that the evolution of "living things" proceeds at a much higher speed. And not only that: In ever decreasing periods of time not only an ever increasing amount is created, from a purely *quantitative* point of view. No, everything is simultaneously growing more and more complex and more complicated. At first, within rather long time periods, then gradually increasingly faster in shorter time periods, a growing number of new forms of life are created and incredibly many *qualitative* leaps are seen.

Whereas the evolution of the universe from the start up to the creation of our solar system took many billions of years, only about half a billion years have passed between the start of life on this Earth and today.
And while the development of hooves took evolution about 40 million years, it only took a few hundred thousand years, perhaps even less, for the human brain to develop although it is far more complex.

54

As I already mentioned above, humans today differ tremendously from their ancestors in the Stone Age, but this does not necessarily apply to the hardware, i.e. the brain.

Especially the "spiritual" qualities, i.e. the "immaterial" ones, and in general terms, the "informational things" are so different from those of our ancestors. It is interesting to recognise that even now – with us humans – evolution has obviously by no means come to a standstill:

In the course of many millions of years, the individual being initially did *not develop independently* of its species. Evolution rather always encompassed the entire collective. But it changed its aim and purpose relatively early on; some birds and, above all, numerous mammals can obviously start to mature individually. A heron, for example, can learn just by observing how children attract fish by feeding them. The herons then steal leftover breadcrumbs from the children, not, however, to eat them but as a means to an end. For them the bread turns into bait. Then they wait for a fish to try and snap it. Then they strike. But only the herons, which have observed the feeding of the fish, are able to do this. They have individually learned something because they also understood the interrelation. Thus they can now develop further individually by means of their mind (or generally speaking: the spirit).

Thus they differ from other members of the same species. In the same way, evolution has long since taken place with individual human beings. By no means is evolution a collective affair any longer, as some political dreamers with misconceptions have repeatedly been trying to make us believe for the last 200 years.

Nevertheless, humans develop *individually*, detached from all other living beings. And this development has long been a *purely spiritual* one.

With their individual progresses they become role models for others. This enables others to follow suit, so that the collective can also participate. This is what we term culture and cultural development. Cultural development can only grow if the further developed individuals are prepared to "take along" their neighbours who may be lagging in their progress. This is then exactly the essential basis for their own further development. *Cultural development is thus primarily not a collective matter.*

Cultural development can certainly not be controlled "from above" on the basis of "collective delusions".
In fact, only at the beginning does the collective play a major role in the evolution of life. But the stronger especially the spiritual development grows and the further it progresses the more the collective recedes into the background. Those who do not understand this today and even loudly preach the opposite should first work hard on themselves, since they have obviously not yet gone through some very important stages in their own spiritual development. However, they will be bound to do exactly that – and if possible in the "here and now"; otherwise their future will be very traumatic for a while. I will come back to this in more detail later.

Cultural progress is thus initially the result of an ideally broad-based individual development, in particular on a spiritual level.
The required hardware for this hardly changes, but should it do so, then only to a small, microscopic degree by providing a few faster, optimised access options "for the spirit using them" due to improved wiring.
The spiritual evolution of the individual is, therefore, the decisive aspect and the topic of our time.
This alone also facilitates any development towards ever more complex and complicated forms of life by better and intensified interaction with its hardware. Of course, this is certainly not possible in a material way: "Electromagnetic access" is, therefore, impossible. Physics is right to opt out here.
However, somehow the universe also emerged once, perhaps by way of a big bang or, as I believe, it has emerged multiple times over long periods and it still continues to do so, solely due to the impact of information.
The Gospel of St John is probably correct when it says: "In the beginning was 'logos'", translated by *Martin Luther (1483-1546)* as "the

word". This might be the exact equivalent of the physicists' "quantum fluctuations", since "logos" is also a synonym for "information".

In a similar way as information generates the formation of matter, it has also a direct effect on the brain and generates an evolution of the spiritual or, in general, the "informational". This then leads to an accelerated evolution of all living bodies which are being increasingly provided with a spirit.

From a certain moment onwards, the evolution of physical but *living* things thus stands out from that of all *"non-living"* things:

Initially very gradually and hardly noticeably, but then slowly accelerating with growing speed and finally increasingly fast, evolution attains a completely new level: the level of the purely "informational" or "spiritual".

At the same time, the purely physical recedes into the background

Evidently physical but "non-living" things already possess this second side of the coin, the polar-symmetrical side of the informational, right from the start. Even planets and entire galaxies somehow seem to "know" how to move. And, as I already explained, smallest particles which are interconnected or entangled, as it is termed in physics, even over enormous distances can always be determined in the same way; because whenever you capture or measure one of the two "entangled" forms, then you can only capture or measure the other form – regardless of wherever it is in the universe.

This "knowledge" is an integral part of the "informational", i.e. of the non-physical, other side of this world.

This side alone determines what, when, how and where something is basically possible and can harmonise or exist together with something else. This is the basis of all fundamental key data in the entire universe, as we can experience, measure and observe it. It is based on elementary mathematical logic and simple geometric relationships. All this is also "logos".

Initially and in the course of immense periods of time, "physical" but "non-living things" developed. They too have an "informational" component, which determines the framework and influences the physical side. Simultaneously, it undergoes its own evolution. If at some point the maturity level of the "informational" ("spiritual") surpasses that of the exclusively physical, then this leads to a new and higher order and structure: "life" emerges. This means that physical things emerge which are simultaneously also *"living"* things, since "life" is "continuous", which is not a physical property but an exclusively "spiritual or informational property".

The physics of physical but "non-living" things has *no continuity at all* – nowhere and not even if people like to suggest otherwise by invoking special interpretations. [27]

Physics is the science of the "discontinuous" or, according to *Max Planck,* of the "quantised", i.e. the doctrine of the smallest particles or quanta. Mathematics alone establishes the connections and gives them continuity. Physics depicts this and thus reflects really existing, elementary-mathematical principles.

Therewith a very interesting aspect arises: If the universe really emerged 13.8 billion years ago with a big bang, as the dogmatic teaching today mostly suggests, what was there before and what was it made of if cosmic space did not exist at the time of this big bang?

This question implies, of course, that cosmic space constitutes some kind of physical quality, or that it is something physical.

To me, this seems to be a fundamental mistake, for, as anyone can experience, in the same way as a particle of light or a "photon", cosmic space must already primarily possess continuity. It cannot be fragmented or quantised or simply discontinuous.

This is why a light particle is credited with the double nature of being "wave and particle simultaneously", which is hardly understandable from a purely physical point of view. This is supposed to effect the continuity of space.

---

[27] Example: wave-particle dualism of light, see former chapter.

No, our cosmic space has always been continuous because it is not a physical space. Rather, it should be understood as always having been exclusively spiritual or, generally speaking, "informational".

We can imagine it as being practically *a four-dimensional coordinate system growing into infinity.*[28]

And, therefore, "matter" may have been continuously created "within and with it", i.e. not just once due to a big bang. Accordingly, the cause for the emergence of matter seems indeed to be what physicists believe in: so-called quantum fluctuations. They are invisible and have no physical properties. Ultimately, they are nothing more than the "information" of a really existing, continuously growing cosmic space which we term the "universe". But it is of exclusively "informational" nature and has thus always and everywhere been a *continuous* space.

We must simply realise that continuity is always a characteristic of the "immaterial" and that this also applies to the cosmic space which we call universe. Thus it should become evident to all of us that life cannot be a product of the physical world either; for life is continuous. It goes without saying, therefore, that life is another characteristic of the "informational".

In other words it can be said: Life is a *spiritual force* – or also: life is the *force of the spirit or of the spiritual.*

We term the *force on the physical side energy:*

The famous physicist *Albert Einstein (1879-1955)* once said accurately: *"Energy is frozen matter."*

Similarly, we can say that *"spirit"* is a kind of *"bonded life".*

Spirit becomes evident by "complex information clusters" developed in the course of life.

At the beginning everything "informational" matures step by step and, to a large extent, still parallel to the development of the physical, as long as it has not yet come alive. With the onset of life this parallel

---

[28] For father details please refer to my numerous earlier books published since 1999.

development ceases. Slowly at first and hardly perceptible, but soon with accelerating speed it moves away from synchrony and develops its own systems.

At the beginning of life – characteristic for everything in physics – chance initially determines here what develops when and how. The term "mutation" has been coined for this evolution of life. However, the potency of coincidence – and thus also that of all mutations – decreases with the increasing maturity of the informational, very slowly at first, but then with accelerating speed.

The higher the spirituality of life becomes, the more successfully it resists coincidence and in the end it even assumes more and more influence over its own evolution by means of its spiritual level – even interactively. Thus, the term "epigenetic", coined a long time ago, gains a new quality – and finally also a reasonable explanation.

Interactions on all Levels

So, in the course of immense periods of time, even pure coincidence always provokes a completely new and simultaneously higher order. Time helps in this process, but inconceivably long periods of time are necessary. In contrast, the evolution of life proceeds rapidly on the fast track:

Especially coincidences are gradually playing an ever less important role. On the contrary, they would often rather harm and constrain any development which has adopted such a new and unbelievably accelerated speed. That is why nature more often than not has tried to eliminate them outright and has also installed ingenious protections. I was the first to describe an absolutely crucial safety device in my book "Key to Eternity" (2000): Nature provides such a safety device by means of a genetic placeholder code. In this way, very many mutations are rendered harmless from the outset and thus also drastically reduces the risk of serious diseases such as cancer (see also Part 2, examples from chemistry and biology).

Nature utilises *networking* to supersede the role of the immense periods of time needed to create order out of chaos by means of pure coincidence.

Information can be widely distributed in ever shorter periods of time by creating enormous networks within the new living systems. Random events are merged very quickly and are processed by means of new and especially adapted control centres. This in turn induces ever more targeted responses in an ever broader spectrum in ever shorter time. Coincidence will certainly still make its "star appearance". But it is just as likely to be switched off or neutralised more and more often. These control centres will soon become increasingly more sophisticated and they will assume more tasks and new and more specialised functions. New and increasingly higher levels of control and decision making will emerge over time due to cooperation and numerous combinations.

What do you spontaneously think of?

It is well known that there are immense networks in the world of plants: For example, there are huge colonies of fungi which rapidly spread underground helping each other very successfully by exchanging all kinds of nutrients but, above all, also very useful *information* concerning attacking pests, for example. This benefits all resident forms of life. It is termed *symbiosis.*

In the world of animals up to humans, other and completely new forms of cooperation emerge in addition to symbioses in an "area between beings", but now also on an individual basis: A more or less gigantic and widely ramified system for information transfer is created in every individual being.

I am talking about a nervous system with a rapidly growing number of central switching points. These interconnect and form larger units and control centres and they specialise more and more in very specific tasks.

This is how the "central nervous system" (CNS) develops.

The CNS is the suitable physical trellis for the spiritual while it is simultaneously still growing itself, and, for a long time, these two develop in parallel.

Gradually, however, the CNS reaches new and ever higher levels. An important aspect must be pointed out here:

The evolution of the purely physical seems to have been a path with many dead ends, with some somersaults and temporary regressions, i.e. it has been *cyclical.* In contrast, the evolution of the CNS must be considered as having been a strictly linear and consistently upwards pointing process.

This can even be substantiated anatomically: There is a discrepancy in the spine between the evolutionary maturation of the spinal cord and the bony encasement. The spinal cord only starts above the first lumbar vertebra. Below this point there are only nerves – which evolved much earlier – so that it is relatively safe for surgeons to carry out lumbar punctures and block anaesthesia at this point.

Thus, the spinal cord also reflects the phylogenetic development of humans (phylogeny). For long periods of time, communication was possible solely via peripheral lines, which were later followed by small inserted switching points.

At first, the "spiritual potential" still grows slowly and mostly in parallel with the necessary physical resources.

Gradually, however, it starts to stand out and diverges, initially growing still very slowly, but later increasingly fast and finally exponentially. This is why 400 generations of humans have been sufficient to propel us from Stone Age into today's age of modern technology, at first only gradually but later at breathtaking speed.

In contrast, the brain, the physical basis of our spiritual development or, as I often call it the physical equipment pool, has hardly changed at all during this time. In addition, the evolution of the CNS promotes new abilities to surface:

In retrospect we could perhaps draw the following comparison: The early nervous system was comparable to an ancient valve radio.

Although we could receive useful information it was still minimalist in its performance and, of course, yet unable to interact.

With the actual CNS, the system already became much more complex: While the early CNS was comparable to the latest technology craze in the 1950s, when radio cabinets with ten-record changers and CRT television sets for the lounge became fashionable, the modern CNS is now capable of new, more diverse and better skills. The variety of television programmes also grew in spite of there being only a few television broadcasting stations at the time.

Of course, this is only an analogy; because nature is in every aspect vastly superior to us humans, whatever we do.

The television set as a mere receiving device developed into a PC at some point, initially without direct access to the outside world. But it was possible to work actively with it and not just consume. The result of such work could then be printed out, for example.

Later, telephone modems were developed. So the first interactive, even paper-free access to an "external data sphere" was made possible even if it was still rather troublesome and restricted. There was still very little information available about it, but rules as to how to work and format it already existed. It took quite some time to accumulate useful data: The internet was born.

Today we use it constantly and worldwide. Without the internet many people could no longer get by. Its wealth of data has grown exponentially due to global interactions and has long since become unfathomable. Almost all of us use it and we create our own password-protected area, the *intranet* – or, in other words – our own "web within the web".

Let us compare this now to the spiritual development or, generally speaking, to the "development of the informational" of *all* living beings: Here as well, the suitable devices had to be created gradually.

These are represented by the CNS which started with simple nerves, and later developed growing numbers of initially small switching points which then grew ever larger and increased in number until they eventually matured to highly complex switching units and central processing units.

Our human brain represents an at least temporary peak in this development. But even if the development of the hardware has perhaps been completed, the development of potential possibilities is still far from being so.
We humans have probably only reached a preliminary tip of the iceberg, since our CNS is at least a sufficiently matured, strictly hierarchically organised and centrally controlled equipment pool for consciousness and self-awareness. With this we can now operate interactively and we can become aware of it.
On this level of maturity, our brain seems to be more efficient than that of any other living being on our Earth.
Now that our CNS has reached this level of development we are able to consciously create our own "intranet" within a "universal spiritual internet" *(outernet)*.
Even without new hardware we are able to expand it consistently and to recognise it always as our very own.
Not only do we have, but we *are* now our own "cloud" and thus we always and everywhere become aware of our own personality, within which this cloud can exist.

The enormous networking, especially in the brain, is the basis of an "informational evolution": Thus, everything spiritual, the "informational", develops, slowly at first and relatively parallel to the maturing hardware "brain". With the growing network it becomes, of course, faster and it expands. However, soon there is an ever widening gap: Despite unchanged anatomy, the informational, i.e. the spiritual, keeps growing faster, even exponentially.
An unbelievably vast network is developed in the brain of humans. Nevertheless, this does *not* support the widely spread thesis of our zeitgeist gurus according to which our brain ultimately produces our spirit and that this is only a coincidental "epiphenomenon" of matter.

Those who talk about this in such hackneyed clichés overlook a most astounding anatomical fact:

There are certain structures for the transmission of information within the nervous system. We call such docking points "synapses". That synapses also exist in the brain was discovered by the Australian brain researcher *John Eccles (1903-1997),* who is for me still the greatest brain researcher today. He was awarded the Nobel Prize for this in 1963.

There are more than 100 billion neurons in the brain and many more connections between them via their extensions, the *neurites* and *dendrites* – and thus also countless synapses.

However, by far the most of these synapses in the brain, probably trillions, have a dead end and sit at the top of the cerebral cortex pointing outwards (known as *spike synapses*).

There they end and, in contrast to "normal synapses", they do not connect with anything else.

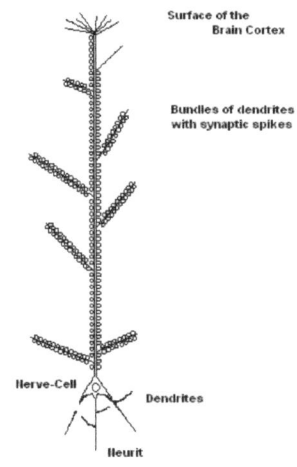

Fig. 9 Neuron near the brain surface

In the 1970s, Eccles compared them to countless small satellite dishes reaching upwards (Fig. 9).

Even back then Eccles had the idea that "information" from an "environment", which is imperceptible for our senses but nevertheless "really existing", could actively influence our brain from the outside via these free spike synapses, in the same way as TV programmes, distributed by numerous satellites, are received by satellite dishes today.

It follows: TV programmes constitute also very complex information which is present in the environment when broadcasted: If we just take

a radio instead of a TV set, however, then we cannot see anything. If we take a television set, which is "phase-shifted" to other signals, we cannot see anything either – in spite of a suitable satellite dish.
Everything must be perfectly synchronised.

Sadly, Eccles was not taken seriously with his idea:
On the one hand, such ideas did not fit into the world view, neither then nor today. Hence they were ridiculed then and still are now.
Should any evidence support these ideas then they are antagonised. We experience this today first-hand again.
On the other hand, physicists disagree. They are quite right with their opinion that an electromagnetic interaction with the brain must be ruled out. Yet, this should indeed be the case. Once again they were in line with the zeitgeist then and they still are now.
However, if today physicists almost unanimously explain the birth of our universe as being a coincidental event after the big bang caused by quantum fluctuations 13.8 billion years ago, then Eccles' considerations should definitely be taken up again:
Coincidences and random events must indeed occur – a fact, which is, of course, not contradicted by physicists and cosmologists. For all advocates of the zeitgeist coincidences are the core of every evolution, for that of our universe as well as for that of all life. This seems indeed to be the case even if esoterics usually do not agree.
Coincidences are chaotic. However, as Benoit Mandelbrot was already able to show, every coincidence generates (strict) order again at some point and, if necessary, after immense periods of time.
It seems that the evolution of *"non-living"* matter, and thus of all cosmic structures such as galaxies, suns and planets, can be explained adequately in this way. Thus, fantasy and other ideas seem unnecessary for many people to explain "life".
However, since it remains a fact that we know nothing at all about 95% of the universe today, this attitude verges for me on stagnancy in thinking. For that very reason I would wish that all cosmologists would have more fantasy especially today, since their current explanations resulting in "dark matter" and "dark energy" seem rather dull and

unimaginative. Furthermore, I am convinced both explanations are also most certainly wrong.

If we classify our zeitgeist as what it really is, namely rubbish, then we are free to think along very simple, plausible and conclusive –new – lines.

In living systems, coincidences are being "replaced" by increasingly complex interconnections, gradually at first and with growing speed later. A higher organisation of such interconnections is achieved by the development of central nervous systems (CNS) over long periods of time.

In the course of time, it becomes more and more important to rein in coincidence effectively in living systems; because coincidences, here termed mutations, are usually harmful. The rapid evolution of life could still tolerate coincidences at the beginning and may even have needed them as a starting condition. In the course of time, however, it became a steadily growing importance to eliminate them consistently.

Thus, it follows: Information has an effect on all living systems and it is the key to a new, better view of the world.

But how can we visualise the effect of "information", i.e. of *"non-physical"* structures, on *physical* structures?

On the one hand, several generations have already failed to explain this. This does not irritate me. On the other hand, physics is right when it says that *electro-magnetic interactions* – for example with our brain – are unthinkable.

Then there must be a different way for information to affect the brain. And this seems to be the case.

Such "informational" or "spiritual" influences evolved only gradually and then started to grow rapidly. The further evolution progressed, the stronger they grew, and they also became increasingly faster, more and more controlled and steadily more purposeful.

It seems that at the beginning of everything – even though not after one *single* big bang 13.8 billion years ago, but rather after frequent and ever "smaller circumstances of birth" causing the emergence of cosmic matter – the meanwhile "famous" quantum fluctuations started the process. They take us to the border between matter and information: Since these quanta, "sloshing back and forth", i.e. fluctuate, have no rest mass, so they are basically not matter, just as photons are actually not matter either.

Everything arises thereof – however, again and again induced by pure coincidence.

Let us now take a giant leap almost across the entire 13.8 billion years from the beginning of the universe, according to current opinion, up to us humans.

Humans now have a brain with hundreds of billions of nerve cells, hundreds of billions of interconnections and trillions of synapses in between. Electrical impulses are transmitted from one nerve to another or – in the peripheral body – to a target organ via these synapses.

This is almost always facilitated by chemical substances such as messenger substances, transmitters, or *neurotransmitters* in the CNS. They are released by small so-called vesicles near the ends of synapses.

There are many billions of infinitesimally small nerve endings (dendrites) blindly pointing upwards to the cerebral cortex, which are studded with trillions of such *vesicles*, accurately arranged in a vesicular grid like in an egg carton.

They protrude outwards like small satellite dishes.

They contain transmitters. When a vesicle bursts, the transmitters are released and can trigger some kind of reaction, e.g. the transmission of a nerve impulse.

It is exactly here that the key to *non-electromagnetic* effects may lie: Purely *"informational effects"* possibly occur on these vesicular grids. And this is not magic.

The incredible abundance of cross-links, having been developed in the course of immense periods of time, is both the key and the reason for everything. It explains everything in such a simple way, as I have predicted:

Let us start with simple physics again: Coincidence plays the leading role in the world of physical but *"non-living"* bodies. But even then ever higher orders emerge. However, immense, often agonisingly long periods of time are necessary. As long as no (living) observer watches closely, it does not seem to matter, of course.

However, as can be proven beyond doubt, evolution grows faster and faster, however, as soon as "life" appears. Matter is created in this process which evidently now develops structures which are capable of helping to accelerate evolution. Simultaneously matter itself keeps developing further and further. Coincidence, as a possibly agonisingly slow engine, interferes and must be restrained. Thus, its disadvantages, such as mutation-related damage, are clearly mitigated, particularly since they would also restrict accelerated evolution, of course.

Imagine you were living in the 18th century, long before radio waves were discovered and before engines were invented to make travel faster than by a horse-drawn carriage or sailing ships.

You wanted to invite many friends and relatives to a big party. Meanwhile, some of them are scattered all over the world, maybe due to expeditions for research or trade purposes. I immediately think of the famous German natural scientist *Alexander von Humboldt (1769-1859).*

Of course, most of your family and friends live within easy reach or some distance away. You want all of them to come.

You would certainly have to start sending out invitations many months, perhaps over a year before the event, by pony express, messengers, trade missions, and so on. And whether everyone could be contacted would be very uncertain. In any case, everything would have to be exactly planned a very long time in advance and various methods would have to be taken. Long lead times would be necessary.

How would it be today?

You plan who should come, draft a personalised circular email inviting them all and in only a few minutes everything is done. The recipients are in the know even if they live on other continents. Those you cannot reach by email, you can probably phone or you could send a message and in some cases you could even send a letter by our good old snail mail. You could thus plan your festivity a few days or at most a few weeks in advance, but you would never need many months or even a year or more.

You would only need a very short lead time.

All this is the result of modern communication methods based on gigantic and also very fast networks.

A comparison between the evolution of *"non-living"* matter and that of *"living"* matter with its rapidly growing network within the CNS shows not exactly the same but a quite similar picture.

In the world of physics these interconnections now seemingly eliminate the "separateness" – or the "discontinuity" – of all *"non-living"* physical bodies".

In doing so, these interconnections act like illusionists; they do not really do it, hence I added "seemingly".

With the development of gigantic networking systems, "physics" imitates a "continuity" which is actually not its inherent quality. For the real "continuity", the "living", "spiritual" or "informational", this is sufficient to be reflected in the physical world, without becoming aware of its illusionary appearance.

In reality, it is only an illusion created by an interface between the "informational or spiritual world" and the "physical world" after all the necessary "systems" have matured.

You could compare this to a movie consisting of many individual pictures. The illusion of continuity which we know as film can only be created if these individual pictures follow one another fast enough, i.e. in rapid succession. In fact, however, the pictures remain discontinuous since they are based on physical matter. Due to the speed of succession and correct "networking", i.e. the pictures must follow one another rapidly and must be arranged in the correct order, we experience a discontinuous sequence of pictures as a continuous film.

However, only we perceive this as a film since we as living beings and as such always also part of another world are, of course, used to "continuity". From a physical point of view, i.e. from the world of "non-

70

living", physical bodies (or matter), there is no film, but there are only discontinuous pictures proceeding in rapid succession, no matter how fast.

Having said that, hence it follows:

Time and space are two "interfaces": Both are positioned between the physical (purely material) and the informational (spiritual) world and can themselves possess both aspects.

When we speak of "infinite time" or "eternity", we always mean the "informational aspect", which also refers to an infinite space. According to the current view of most physicists, the universe appears to be such an infinite space. I agree without reservation and add: This is just how it is. From this point of view, space and time are infinite. Consequently, however, they are not of physical nature, since infinity does not exist (nowhere) in *physics*.

On the other hand, there are, of course, countless "finite bodies" and thus "finite spaces". They are bodies and spaces which are located within an *infinite* space surrounding them. Finite bodies with finite spaces are also of finite time, just like every living being inevitably is.

But all living beings themselves contain the two informational characteristics: "life" and "spirit". So they are simultaneously beings of the other, the "informational side" of this world, which is characterised by infinity of time and space.

All "non-living" bodies, i.e. simple matter, carry an "informational aspect" as well, of course, which also makes them infinite in time and space. However, this is only simple information which is unable to become aware of itself.

They are. Or generally speaking: lifeless matter *is (it exists)*.

Living beings, on the other hand, are characterised by *their existence and their development* whereby the following applies: The higher the spiritual level of the living being, the more the *main focus is placed on development.* This is especially true for us humans. Within the framework of *their development, all individuals* achieve the potential of becoming aware of *themselves* and thus *recognise* their actual position within the evolution of the world. In so doing, they leave the sphere of being, which *infinitely exists* merely in time and space. They rather become *conscious* and *active* participants in the infinite development of time and space. But this also applies to ourselves, which also means that we, too, must become aware of our immediate responsibility for "ourselves and those around us" and must take over responsibility accordingly. This also makes each one of us the architect of our own happiness.

I will come back to this in the next chapter.

Another example:

Do you take part in the lottery? In the German version with 6 correct numbers out of 49, you already have the choice of almost 14 million possibilities even without taking the bonus number into account. Thus your chances of winning the jackpot are only very small. It seems very unlikely that you will choose exactly these 6 *"right numbers"* which are later "drawn".

Let us now assume that in one vesicle grid of the countless synapses in the brain, which look like satellite dishes and have a blind ending, there are 100 vesicles, stacked like eggs in a carton. Of these only 10 are emptied at random, not specific ones as in the lottery, to induce the entire grid to be completely emptied at once. This should then trigger an initial electrical impulse.

If we apply this and start calculating, then there would be over 17 trillion possibilities, and an extremely high probability.

In contrast to the lottery, in this metaphor it is completely irrelevant *which vesicles* burst, as long as there are 10 out of 100 that do. If it were also irrelevant for the lottery, which 6 numbers we choose, then we would all be millionaires every week. Wouldn't that be great?

In the vesicle grids it would suffice for only 10 random ones out of the supposed 100 vesicles per grid to burst and release transmitters to trigger an electrical impulse.

Applied to our metaphor this would mean: Due to this extremely high probability of triggering a process, a single thought alone could target the brain effectively by randomly triggered quantum processes.

Therefore, it becomes necessary to curb this process somewhat:

72

So it would be better, if it were necessary that a certain number of vesicles in several such grids would burst *simultaneously* in one or several nerves (neurons), thus releasing their transmitters. With this ludicrously high probability, which I assume here, even that would not be a big problem; it would only raise the hurdles to some degree.

With such a high probability of triggering a process, it would still be easy to achieve this – and so it seems to be, as we experience ourselves every day.

Let us further assume now that as many as 1,000 neurons or so would be needed to be *briefly and simultaneously triggered* in this manner, just for lifting an arm, for example, as the German engineer *Ralf Otte,* Director of the Institute for Artificial Intelligence and Automation Systems at the TH (Technical College) Ulm, Germany, wrote in his contribution to my conference transcript 2018.[29]

Only then the relevant centres in the cerebral cortex (motor cortex and others) would set our arm in motion as requested – and other processes too would perhaps be carried out now.

In a neuronal network like that within our brain *all* such neurons are now interconnected. Let us now also assume that triggering 100 random neurons *simultaneously* would be sufficient in this example to "fire" *all* 1,000 nerves *at the very same moment,* then there would be $6,3 \times 10^{139}$ possibilities for triggering processes and thus presumably far more than there are atoms in our universe according to current knowledge.

Hence, the remote possibility of a simultaneous excitation of several nerves by pure chance, due to an extremely high number of nerves and their interconnections, turns into an almost "deterministic necessity" to trigger an excitation.

Information or, more precisely, pure thoughts without physical substrate can have effects on physical structures *without any electromagnetic interaction* whatsoever, as long as they are

---

[29] Otte, R., (2018) „Physikalische Grundlagen des Geistes" (engl. „Physical Basics of the Spirit") in „Schnittstelle Tod -Sind Religionen religiös und Wissenschaften wissend?", NDE Conference Transcript 2017, published in German only

appropriately configured for this. The CNS has suitable structures for this. Evolution has persistently *developed them further* at all times in a *linear* manner. At the same time, everything is strictly compatible downwards, a fact which modern hardware and software components should definitely take as an example.

The current zeitgeist still has no room for things which go beyond physics and are thus of "metaphysical nature".
One of the apparently *"forbidden subjects"* is, for example, the conviction that our mind could also exist independently of the brain. The idea that our "self-personality" does not need to be connected to the brain is certainly also part of this just like many other ideas. Likewise, there is no room in this world view for my firm conviction that our death *cannot at all be our end*, which I strongly commend to you here, because death only refers to the finite physical structures within their respective current constellations. But even the smallest parts of physical systems already possess "information". Although this also can never disappear – in such complex living beings as us humans it would nevertheless already mean "death", since its individually scattered existence would have hardly anything in common with a '"survival".
More highly developed living beings, however, also possess more highly evolved, "complex information clusters". Our personality is an excellent example for this. And, of course, these survive in their incomparably higher developed complexity.

If this be the case, of which I am completely convinced, then it must also have immense consequences – that is to say for *each and every one of us.* This applies particularly to *our personal behaviour as an expression of the development of our personality in the "here and now".* The *structures of our personality, configured in the "here and now", as well as the specific actions we thus exhibit in the "here and now", are then also the determining basis for our further life after the moment which others will then define as "our death".*

This moment will lead all individuals – and from their respective points of view without any discontinuity – to a completely new "higher life".

The consequences for each one of us are enormous and will have a massive impact on everyone for an incalculable length of time. What it will be like and for how long it will last, depends solely on our actions in the "here and now". It is irrelevant what we believe or what we believe in here. The only determining factors are our actions. The appropriate degree of personal responsibility is required. Just how high the appropriate degree is, depends on the individual's position in life.

People who are tied down by the current zeitgeist will have a hard time. But they too must decide, now!

Otherwise they may be (continue to be?) inclined to make many mistakes in the "here and now" towards "themselves and their neighbours", which they will come to regret and must try to correct individually without exception.

Conclusion and my Credo

Meanwhile, I have been convinced for decades that I receive, regularly and especially at very salient points in my life, indications "from somewhere", which are partly overt, partly rather discreetly concealed. Often I have not understood them, and in some cases I even resisted these inputs. Unfortunately, I then had to realise that this was wrong in most cases, in some cases even wrong and irreversible. Fortunately enough, I could usually rescind such wrong decisions. Today I am much more careful in this respect and keep an eye on such indications.

Some people speak of "gut feeling" in such cases. But this does not really get to the core of the matter. It is more than that and it seems by no means to be just a product of my own imagination or pure fantasy.

At present, we are experiencing an ineffable crisis with the Corona virus, an unprecedented event for decades. Despite the many "expert opinions of scientists" which are quickly and widely spread in the media, it seems to me that this can neither be adequately explained with medical arguments, nor can it be clearly and comprehensively proven by data and facts. Numerous politicians and an army of "medical journalists" seem to be rather self-important and far too often resistant to advice.

Even when this viral disease takes unfortunately a severe course in many cases and even ends fatally, it is by no means as aggressive as often described, at least from a statistical point of view. Only relatively few people who come into contact with the virus are taken seriously ill and must be treated in hospital. If at all, it affects mainly old people, especially those with serious pre-existing conditions. As we know, the average age at death of those affected is also in Germany far above the average life expectancy, especially in the case of men, who are somewhat more frequently affected by severe courses.

In consequence of the outbreak of this disease, some countries have reacted with excessive, medically hardly justifiable and often even legally untenable, unlawful and, it seems, only actionist measures.

The true extent of these actions and reactions will probably remain incalculable for many years to come. The result will presumably be simply disastrous for entire groups of society, many branches of industry and for following generations. Unfortunately, the resulting new and massive problems in many countries and for their citizens worldwide are almost disrespectfully described today as "collateral damage". However, especially this collateral damage will probably by far exceed all the problems which are directly caused by the disease itself.

It is no coincidence that some of our contemporaries even associate the disease with the beginning of a new era which does not bode well.

Well-known novels such as "1984" by the British author *George Orwell (1903-1950)* or "Brave New World" by the British author *Aldous Huxley (1894-1963)* seem to be reflected in these reactions, perhaps rightly so.

Many citizens of this world today see themselves to be powerless at the mercy of self-appointed elites with a self-image which is very often based on immense material possessions alone. They believe themselves to have no leverage against these elites. This is how myths are quickly created which are based on some crude ideas of current and former contemporaries and are woven around entire families or groups.

I do not believe in the success of such ideas, regardless of whether they are only legends anyway or are based on facts. Above all, I do not believe in them because they are the product of humans. Without exception, they are based on the zeitgeist which has been restricted for several centuries by purely materialistic ways of thinking and seeing. Such ideas may, as is often the case, inflict ineffable damage to individuals or even entire societies and throw them back for many years to come – but in the end they will all fail.

The credo of my book is based on notions which initially make it possible to explain the pillars of our world in a throughout compelling and conclusive manner. These notions take us beyond the boundaries of our existence. Taking this into account I always try to reconcile all phenomena, observations and actual events from various disciplines, regardless of how different they may be – without ignoring or disregarding individual issues.

Many phenomena exceed the material and thus the purely physical section of this world. Physics has neither an explanation for infinity nor for continuity. We only know finiteness and discontinuity (quantisation or fragmentation). This is why physicists often must bend over backwards when they have to explain continuity although it is virtually something unphysical and it is utterly impossible to do.

Smallest light particles, so-called photons, are thus explained as being particles and waves simultaneously (wave-particle dualism). The physical part of then described as their "particle character". Particles differentiate themselves from others. They are quantised (discontinuous).

But what is the origin of their wave character, i.e. their continuity?

And if this applies to the smallest particles which account for all matter, why does it not apply to big items such as cupboards, houses or even humans in the same way?

However, if we look into cosmic space, our universe, and if we consider the nature of time and that of all our lives, we find continuity everywhere.

It is similar with the term "infinity".

None of us can really imagine what it means. Large numbers are acceptable up to a certain point, and "a little bit more" could probably also be comprehended. But already a 1 with 100 zeros is virtually incomprehensible. Mathematicians may conjure up a few real examples to illustrate this number. However, even this seems to go far beyond "the edge of all understanding" according to the notions of cosmologists today, since current figures assume a maximum of 10^{89} atoms in the entire universe, which is the equivalent of a number 1 with 90 zeros. *But infinite?*

Nevertheless, the famous German mathematician *David Hilbert*[30] already explained infinity for all ordinal numbers (natural numbers) with the intellectual experiment known as *Hilbert's Hotel*. In the 19th century, the ingenious German mathematician *Georg Cantor*[31] was even able to *prove* in a strictly mathematical way that infinity, in fact, exists, that it is real. And that is not all: there are even an infinite number of such infinities.

For the "ancient Greeks", this was actually a well-known fact.

Admittedly, they did not prove it in a strictly mathematical sense. For them, it was sufficient, simply to consider a circle: They were amazed to discover that, although it was "optically finite", it revealed its second side which proved to be infinite the moment they tried to "determine" it mathematically. For example, no one can calculate the area and circumference of a circle or the volume of a sphere exactly. For this reason we always need the infinite circle number pi (π) which we all know from our school days.

---

[30] David Hilbert (1862-1943). Famous is his image of a "Hilbert space"
[31] Georg Cantor (1845-1918)

But all this is no longer part of "physics", it goes beyond that horizon. A term was also coined for this, the term *"metaphysics"*. However, as is so often the case in science: Something amazing is found and cannot be understood or explained any further by "traditional" methods and knowledge. Then, with a new term, one simply invents a drawer in which to hide this problem. However, this does not solve the questions, it just sounds as if it does.

The credo of my present book thus leads in a completely different direction which should, however, encourage every single individual to be full of hope and optimism.
This is true, at least as long as humans are peace-loving and prepared to master their lives lovingly and with a good heart. More to this later.

My credo even leads to the great hope of being able to construct a broad and conclusive chain of argumentation by compelling circumstantial evidence. Even if it *cannot offer conclusive evidence in a strictly scientific sense*, it could certainly serve as prima facie evidence. And it should (finally) be able to rid the world of a lot of nonsense, which has all too often been generated by self-appointed elites and created on the basis of religious or political-ideological attitudes.

Of course, such nonsense is always to their advantage, but simultaneously it is just as often also to the disadvantage of smaller or larger sections of society. Contemporaries exercising such power and their many like-minded collaborators base their chutzpah relentlessly on a false, indeed downright absurd, but contemporary naturalism.
It could well be that one or the other may now regard me and this credo already in the introduction as a "dangerous kamikaze driver on the motorway heading in the wrong direction". However, in doing so, they overlook that in fact they themselves are actually the drivers heading in the wrong direction. And they will bitterly regret this one day, unless they learn to "recognise and rethink" their attitude in the "here and now".

I already illustrated in a "belletristic-easy-to-read" way in my currently only novel "Our Key to Eternity" (2015) that *all individuals for themselves* must and they also do set the course *for their own future* in the "here and now".

My credo is based on a wide-ranging and conclusive chain of evidence which has grown over several decades. It has led me almost compellingly and unmistakably to the clear conviction that our death "here" is *not* simultaneously the end of our "individual personality".
From the perspective of individuals who "die here", their life continues *instantaneously and without any interruption while maintaining all the attributes of their hitherto grown personality.*

Especially in this day and age, it may be difficult for many to digest. Nevertheless, it seems to be an irrefutable fact which applies to all individuals, whether they want to believe it or not.
For all individuals, the following seems to be equally true and quite certain, *no matter what and who, where and how they are prepared to believe or not to believe today*:

1) Death is not the end of our personality.

2) For all individuals it continues seamlessly afterwards – and from their perspective without any interruption – with full personality and orientation as well as with all their knowledge – just as they are at the time of their departure here or, better, their transition.

3) All individuals are equipped with a will which is fundamentally free and only limited by the respective environmental conditions ("here" for example, they are mainly met by physical limits).

4) For all Individuals it is crucial *to recognise, to understand and to learn* in the "here and now" that they are bearing a *very personal, individually varying degree of direct responsibility.*

The degree of personal responsibility is strictly graded in accordance with the degree of responsibility the deceased have had in the "here and now", i.e. how much responsibility they had been given or they had assumed. Their responsibility relates to "themselves and their neighbours". This is also the lesson of the Christian "Parable of the Ten Pounds" in the Gospel of Luke (19:12). So, what is it all about?

"A man went to a distant country to have himself appointed king and then to return. So he called ten of his servants and gave them ten mina. 'Put this money to work,' he said, 'until I come back.' When he returned home, he sent for the servants to whom he had given the money, in order to find out what they had gained with it. "The first one came and said, 'Sir, your mina has earned ten more.' "'Well done, my good servant!' his master replied. 'Because you have been trustworthy in a very small matter, take charge of ten cities.' "The second came and said, 'Sir, your mina has earned five more.' "His master answered, 'You take charge of five cities.' "Then another servant came and said, 'Sir, here is your mina; I have kept it laid away in a piece of cloth. I was afraid of you, because you are a hard man. You take out what you did not put in and reap what you did not sow.' "His master replied, 'I will judge you by your own words, you wicked servant! You knew, did you, that I am a hard man, taking out what I did not put in, and reaping what I did not sow? Why then didn't you put my money on deposit, so that when I came back, I could have collected it with interest?' "Then he said to those standing by, 'Take his mina away from him and give it to the one who has ten minas.' "'Sir,' they said, 'he already has ten!'

"He replied, 'I tell you that to everyone who has, more will be given, but as for the one who has nothing, even what they have will be taken away."

This famous parable is unfortunately often misunderstood:
In no way does it call for more business acumen, as some may claim in their ignorance. Rather, it is simply teaching that all individuals must take over responsibility. However, the responsibility is not the same for everyone, but it is graded resulting from the degree of responsibility assumed or assigned in the "here and now".

In a similar way we must consider the saying, often misunderstood today: *"The first will be the last" (Matthew 20:16):*

By "the first" are meant those who act for their own good *at the cost and expense of their neighbours (Hebrew: ha adamah)* in the "here and now". In contrast "the last" are those who waive their claims in favour of their neighbours, in order to help or *truly* serve them. Many politicians promise to serve the people when they take office. However, only a few keep their word later.

For example, managers at the helm of companies also carry a lot of responsibility for their employees. In accordance with this responsibility which they have taken over in the "here and now" they may be found guilty and every single one will have to pay for it after "death".

Therefore, justice is not only an empty phrase.

It exists, and every individual will experience it. Unfortunately, we do not experience justice – or only very rarely – during our life in the "here and now". Those, however, who have burdened themselves with great guilt in the "here and now", may it be that they do not recognise their personal responsibility, or just ignore the actual circumstances of their responsibility to restore justice, will one day regret it very much; because after their so-called death they will be bound to make up for injustice point by point. And sooner or later everyone will succeed. But the way there will then be much stonier, so it would be better to start rethinking already "here".

Once again, we find in these parables – as well as in many near-death experiences, for example – a direct reference to the stern demand for *personal responsibility*.

Repeatedly we find the reference to a *"heavenly justice".* However, there will be *no "heavenly judge".*

To "work off" our own guilt will be our very own duty and will be much more arduous than we here ever expected it to be.

All individuals will be their own judge and each "ego" is unambiguously forced by itself to follow a path which will be more or less arduous, depending on its own past and to ask each one of them individually for

82

forgiveness. That is why we must become aware of this in the "here and now". *There is no way around it for any human being.* For us now, this may sound almost impossible to fulfil, but it will also be a completely new world which we will enter eventually.

This means that Kant's *"categorical imperative"* applies to everyone, which, casually speaking, says: *"Do not do to others what you do not want others do to you."*

The often quoted biblical statement "Love your neighbour as you love yourself" should also been seen in this sense. Both these statements are often not easy to follow.

5) Those who do not meet these personal requirements adequately will have to correct their conduct in future and, if necessary, in a very painful or even agonising manner, until they have redeemed their "guilt" against each and every single one, which resulted from a lack of responsibility towards their neighbours in the "here and now".

Of course, this may sound rather absurd or naïve to many.

Certainly, it may also go beyond the imagination of many when they now think of contemporaries who may have incurred heavy guilt towards millions of their fellow citizens.

But it is neither naïve nor absurd, just because it exceeds our present power of imagination. Many spiritual experiences bear witness to this. And at the same time, this is compellingly supported when compared with the obvious, theoretical principles in various fields of science presented here. Each and every individual will, therefore, be surprised one day and should thus take care and be prepared already in the "here and now".

6) Elementary mathematical logic allows us to recognise that in this universe there are basically two mirror-inverted sides opposing one another ("polar-symmetrical") which *really exist* – just like the two sides of one and the same coin. *This is true for everything and anything.*

Very often, however, many people only recognise one of these two sides in the "here and now" and believe this to be the only really existing one; because they can only *perceive* the materialistic-naturalistic side *with their senses*: All the organ systems necessary for this, are, without exception, themselves of a physical nature. This also applies to all devices and instruments which are created in order to find out more about the world, such as telescopes or microscopes, for example.

But basically, such contemporaries – often even against their better knowledge – do not think any further: However, their daily experience should really give them an indication that there *must be* another side to the coin. And this seems to exist just as real as the side perceived with the senses; for they too recognise their spirit and the wealth of feelings, as well as – in principle – also their reason.

Immanuel Kant (1724-1804) had already worked this out in the 1780s and recognised that "reason" must exist in real terms:

Only with reason can we "process, assess and evaluate" knowledge coming in from all directions and fields of science. By no means, however, is it to be assumed as a "collective reason" although it does indeed really exist, as many of "Kant's emulators" sometimes claim in blatant *stupidity.*

In fact, reason is inherent in *each individual.* And as such, i.e. as the reason bestowed on every one individually, it must be nurtured individually and further developed.

Culture, on the other hand, is a term used for the level of development of a collective. So far so good. However, culture itself can in principle only grow if initially the individual members of a society do so. Only then does the collective grow in the "second row" and subsequently as a whole. Social systems which negate and suppress the individuality of all human beings in favour of collectivism are extremely dangerous aberrations.

They consistently cause great damage to the individual and thus never have a chance of succeeding. Unfortunately, the past 200 years bear ample witness to this. But not everyone learns from the past. Incidentally, this also includes recognising that individuality does not necessarily have anything to do with individualism.

7) The same elementary mathematical logic, however, also forces us to realise that there *must be* a *third reality* beyond these two polar-symmetrical sides of the world which we can generally perceive and recognise. We are unable to describe it in detail. We cannot define it any further. *However, it must be there and it is!* And that is not all. Above and behind everything there is a reality which is simultaneously a primal reality.

From this reality alone everything has emerged, still continues to emerge and proceeds. *Without it, there would be nothing; only through this and with this everything comes into existence.*

For us, it is a new and higher "entity". It is, in the mathematical analogy, equivalent to the world of so-called "imaginary numbers". Although we are able to calculate with them and we know that they exist and that they are even absolutely essential, we cannot even refer directly to them – no matter which way we try.

They remain hidden from our world of real numbers with its two realms of reality, the positive and the negative numbers. And yet, without their existence, we would be unable to operate computers today, for example. Imaginary or "complex numbers"[32] are used today in physics and technology for the precise solution of substantial problems in electrical engineering and aerodynamics, for example, or in quantum physics, when probabilities are to be calculated. Even in music, the "Chladni sound figures" have been known since 1787. They appear when sand is sprinkled onto a plate which is then struck with a violin bow or touched with a vibrating tuning fork: Nodal lines of standing waves are created.

---

[32] See Part 2: The Riemann logarithmic spiral as described in the chapter "Imaginary or Complex Numbers" could be a wonderful analogy for the linear upward development of all information and thus of everything spiritual, while the spiral itself is cyclical (cf. Polar Symmetry of Everything and Everyone)

The higher "entity", which exceeds and pervades everything in our world, has been recognised as existing in reality since time immemorial and has, of course, been given a variety of names.

It is only human then if we try — albeit unreasonably — to imagine it somehow in different images. In Christianity we speak of "God" and we imagine "him" as an old man with a long white beard. We all know that this is naïve and most certainly wrong, but that does not make it bad. Not even the masculine attribute can be correct, more appropriate could at best be my approximation by using *"he + she",* since all polar systems, so also masculine and feminine identifications, first emerge from this entity.

And this higher — spiritual — "Divine Entity" must exist. It is real and possesses its own power. We already experience a lot of this power in the "here and now" and we should pass on as much of it as possible. To do this, we must recognise and comprehend it as a divine power and it is imperative for us to use it: What is meant here is the power of divine *"love"* which is all-embracing and all-pervading and on which everything in this world is based. *Divine Entity is pure love in itself.*

The (Divine) power of love is universal

This is what accompanies all individuals on their personal journey through life. We can ignore it or accept it. It does not force itself upon anyone but it is always present. It accompanies each one of us in the "here and now" and also when the longest part of our individual journey of life has yet to begin: in death.

For a longer or shorter period of time, the subsequent next step of our life will then first and foremost be dedicated to finding the necessary forgiveness for ourselves. Hardly anyone probably is without guilt in the "here and now". We must recognise this and really work through it. There is no judge: we ourselves are challenged; one of the most important insights in the "here and now" is the acceptance of our own free will, whose major task is to recognise and exercise our "personal responsibility".

Of course, this could and should be a task already tackled in the "here and now" of our lives; but many people avoid and dismiss this. All too often, unfortunately, they proceed to inflict harm on others. However, they will regret this later: without exception they will be answerable to themselves and it will become more difficult for them to work off their guilt.

This will be the case because it must be like this; since justice is not an empty phrase. In fact, it will be meted out to each and every individual.
Since all individuals strive to progress on their personal paths and all are obliged to do so, they will do everything they can to come ever closer to achieving their personal goal. This then also includes learning to forgive and to grant forgiveness to others who ask for it.
This happens step by step, or, as it is written in *Matthew 5:38*: *"An eye for an eye, and a tooth for a tooth."*

This is also the actual core message of the next biblical quotation in *Matthew 5:39*. It is just as often misinterpreted: *"If anyone slaps you on the right cheek, turn and offer him the other also"*, this is how it is written and this is exactly how it must be.
This is based on an old Jewish tradition which allowed understanding this statement without problem two thousand years ago: Then as now most people were right-handed. If they were now intent on deeply humiliating someone, they would strike the other person on the right cheek with the back of their right hand.
However, if they were to seek forgiveness later, they would have to pat their opponent's left cheek with their right palm.
To enable this, however, the humiliated person would have to turn the left cheek to the aggressor.

The all important lessons to be learnt for our own further personal path in life beyond our own so-called "death", are to recognise our personal responsibility for everything we do, including the request for forgiveness or the atonement for wrong doings by adopting a new and adapted behaviour as well as attaining the maturity to grant forgiveness and also to be able to love and to accept love.

In contrast, it is irrelevant whether we have a faith in the "here and now" or, if so, what or in whom we believe. The only criterion of any importance is that we act appropriately right now.

Love is the most powerful force in this world. It is the power of the divine or, in a very general and theorising way, the power of the "spiritual entity", which, from our point of view, with absolute certainty really exists, but which cannot at all be described or defined in more detail and which is far above us and superior to us in everything.

It is simultaneously the beginning and the end, as well as the origin and the background of all Being at all times and that throughout eternity.

It is completely irrelevant whether we speak of God, Allah, Manito, Brahman or whoever or whatever.

To discriminate against people of other faiths, to harm them or even to wage war against them for this reason alone is abominable, despicable and, of course, wrong. It is contrary to divine love.

For that very reason, it would be of great benefit if there were more commonality among religions and religious denominations, since it concerns their central subject-matters. They alone give religions their raison d'être.

I received an essay recently from a dear friend about life on board a large sailing cruise ship: *Klaus Müller* had been captain of such ships for 20 years and before that, he was also captain of the legendary three-master *„Alexander von Humboldt"*, which is now de-commissioned and lies at anchor as a hotel ship on the river Weser in Bremen, Germany.

In his essay he wrote, among other things: *"On Sundays at sea I organised a "denominational service", a service without religions. The passengers were invited to attend. Hindus, Buddhists, Muslims, the various Christian denominations, prayed and sang as they used to do in their temples, mosques or churches at home. Jewish guests and Jewish* crew members were also welcome at the service. If there were no Jews on board, I prayed the „Schma Jisrael" in English and in German. It was always a highlight for all of them to present their faith and the spiritual being. I was also asked to organise this service for the crew only. Hearing the Lord's Prayer in Tagalog, Hindu, Russian, German and English evokes a kind of magic.

We should learn to realise that the "Divine Entity" is *not the property* of any one religion and does most certainly not belong to any religious community. It, or simply "God", is there for everyone and stands behind everything in this world. "God" exists in reality and from "Him+Her" everything emerges, including the greatest power in this world.

This power alone should determine all our actions – and, of course, already in the "here and now". Therewith, it should be easy for all of us to master the responsibilities entrusted to us. It is the benchmark for our own future.

God's unlimited mighty power is love. God is love, and love is greater than the entire universe.

Part 2: Backgrounds and Insights

The first BEING and negative and positive number sequences

The most frequent question is probably: Where is the origin of the FIRST BEING?

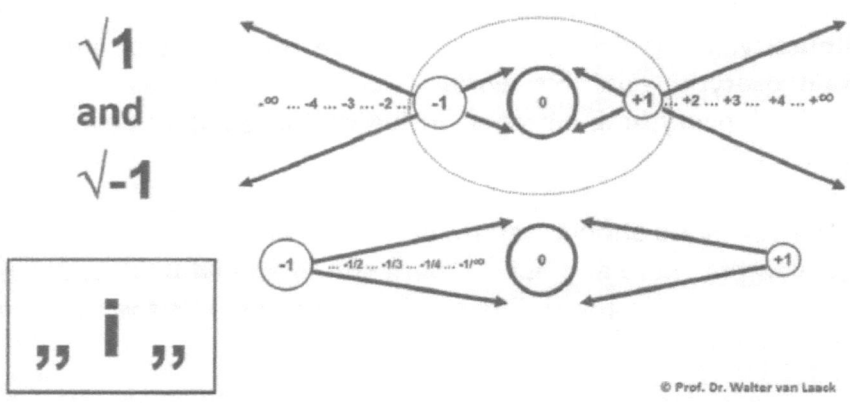

Fig. 10: Origin of the first BEING and its further development.
See the text below:

If you have TWO number worlds which are different from ZERO, mirror-inverted and simultaneously opposed, i.e. polar-symmetrical, you must also be able to perform the same arithmetic operations on *both* of them.

As we all know, we can extract the square root from positive numbers and calculate this with our usual methods. This could result in two positive or two negative numbers. By squaring these numbers again, we arrive at the initial positive number.

However, it is not possible to extract a root from a negative number in the same mathematical way.

In order to extract the square root from a negative number, we must turn to a different perspective which is "out of reach" for us. The result

is then a so-called "imaginary or complex number". It begins with "i" (see Fig 10).
A mathematical equation like $x^2+1=0$ now becomes solvable.

Imaginary or Complex Numbers

Imaginary or complex numbers are calculated from the square root of a negative number. An equation like $x^2+1=0$ becomes solvable. As we all know, we can extract a square root from a positive number and we can calculate it, whereby the result could always be two positive numbers or also two negative numbers. If these numbers are squared we arrive at the initial positive number again.
However, it is not possible to extract a root from a negative number in the same mathematical way.
In order not to dive too deep into further mathematical detail here, I would just ask you to accept in this context the fact that, by using a *"geometric rotation"*, a number can be found which, if multiplied by itself (squared), results in a negative number.
In the simplest case, the imaginary number "i" then turns into "-1" via "i^2".

Viewed geometrically it follows: In this case both numbers "i" are standing in a 90° angle to the real axis. If we now *add up* the two angles, we have an angle of 180°. If we multiply them which each other, then the result is that "i", due to the rotation, falls to the number "-1".
Thus "i" multiplied by "i" gives "-1" and it follows i = √-1.
However, it is misleading to say that imaginary numbers are negative surfaces. They are not.
Imaginary (or complex) numbers are not resulting from surfaces but solely from the rotation.

If complex numbers are multiplied by one another it can cause the rotation to return to the starting point and to go beyond it, like the fingers on a clock.

However, while the fingers on the clock repeatedly point to the same numbers after every 12 hours, this is exactly what is to be avoided with complex numbers.

Each complex number is to remain clearly defined.

This then leads to a superposition of infinitely many surfaces which are arranged in an upwards winding spiral: *Riemann surface of the complex logarithm.* [33] (Fig. 11)

This will be discussed later again in a descriptive analogy.

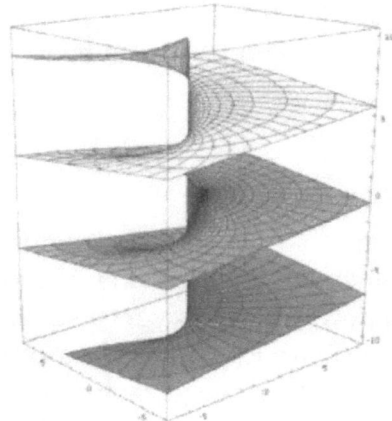

Fig. 11: Spiral of the complex logarithm (Riemann surface)

Polar Symmetry and Infinity

From a purely mathematical point of view, the origin of all "BEING" is thus an "imaginary" or "complex" number "i" (cf. Fig 10).

It MUST exist, but we can only comprehend it in theory. Based on it and with it, both already mentioned number sequences, the negative one and the positive one, emerge successively, and by simply squaring the numbers, they are both also mathematically (arithmetically) real for us.

Applied to the analogy of the two experiential levels of reality "informational world/spirit" and "physical world/matter", it follows: They are also two mirror-inverted and opposing, or polar-symmetrical levels of BEING.

---

[33] Source: https://commons.wikimedia.org/w/index.php?curid=38074912

92

Thus, they are also both based on a *level of BEING* which cannot be described in more detail but which is nevertheless *really existent*, just like the level of the imaginary or complex number "i" in mathematics.

Based on it and with it, the informational or spiritual world develops first, and subsequently from there the physical or material world emerges, i.e. $i^2 = -1$; $(-1)^2 = +1$ (see Fig. 10).

The number ZERO is here also only a *symmetry axis* between the two levels of reality.

The first reality *after "i"*, and thus the level of imaginary or complex numbers, is the level of NEGATIVE numbers. It is the "stronger reality". Based on it and with it the "weaker reality" arises as the level of POSITIVE numbers by squaring.

Because the reverse calculation, the root extraction of positive numbers, can result in positive as well as negative initial values, the negative numbers are the stronger reality.

In the analogy of an "informational, spiritual world" and a "material, physical world", both levels of BEING are *discernible* for us in a figurative sense. However, we are merely able to perceive the "physical world" with our senses, i.e. sensually.

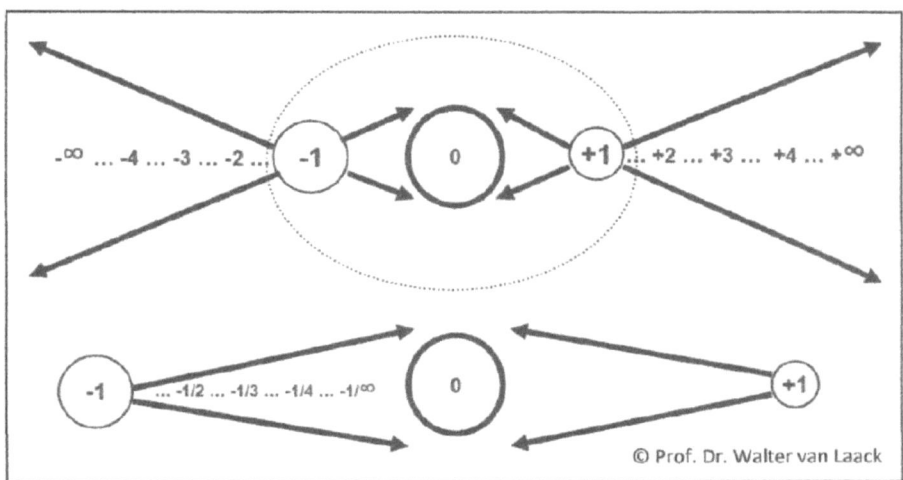

© Prof. Dr. Walter van Laack

Fig. 12: Two levels of "BEING", analogues to negative and positive ordinal numbers

93

Both worlds possess limited and finite aspects, as well as unlimited and infinite ones (Fig. 12).

Although limited by zero and 1, the reciprocals of the natural numbers (ordinal numbers) are nevertheless infinite and lie between these limits.

They are found on the side of the negative numbers as well as on that of the positive numbers, separated by zero as the mirror axis.

The number zero, however, is never reached by either of the two infinite sequences of reciprocals. Infinity thus has "room in finite space" (and in finite time, as I will explain later).

Furthermore, both sides also possess unlimited and simultaneously infinite aspects, symbolised by the two ("normal") infinite number sequences which open up to the right and the left (Fig. 12):

If we now apply the two sequences of positive natural numbers and their reciprocals to my analogy, then it follows:

On the one hand, everything corporeal is spatially limited (three-dimensionally finite) and leads a temporally limited life, i.e. everything is of finite existence.

On the other hand, there is also a second side to the coin for everything and anything:

This second side is infinite and unlimited spatially and temporally. Everything physical also carries this already within itself (Fig. 13).

Each of the two real levels of existence are divided by an interface, characterised by the number "1" (-1 and +1 respectively, Fig. 12). It is equivalent to the *other aspect of BEING*, which is also inherent in everything physical: This is the *"information"* or, in general, its *informational core* (in the adjacent figure depicted as an "informational sphere" within a "physical cube" Fig. 13) on which

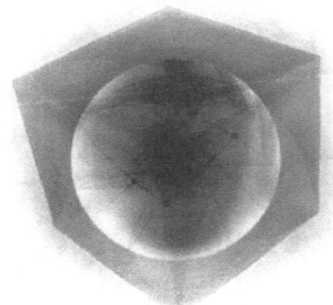

Fig. 13: Informational sphere in a physical cube

94

everything is based. Every physical particle and so every atom as well, possesses an informational core. The more complex physical bodies grow, the more complex their informational nuclei become (clustering).

"Life", as we call it, starts from a certain level of complexity of the informational nuclei – I now term them "informational clusters" or "information clusters".
From a further and higher level of "informational complexity" onwards, we speak of "spirit". However, the development does not stop. It keeps progressing and at some point information clusters emerge which possess "consciousness", and on the next higher level clusters are generated which possess "self-awareness". In us humans, all these "informational clusters" sum up to form our "personality".
At the time of a person's death, it is the equivalent of that person's "soul".

Everything informational or spiritual must, of course, be imagined as being polar-symmetrical in relation to physical matter. Let us consider the brain of a living person, for example: In principle, it is possible to collect an "infinite" amount of information (or spirit) in a space which is admittedly limited by the brain.
Such an accumulation is, however, only possible within a limited, i.e. finite, time (within the lifetime of a person in the "here and now").
Applied to my analogy again, this is symbolised by the respective *reciprocals of the two number sequences,* whereby the negative numbers stand for the "informational" or "spiritual" and the positive numbers for the "physical", i.e. for "physical matter".

Here, the numbers -1 and +1 symbolise the interface "death".
They indicate to us that there is evidently something to proceed to afterwards, for the person concerned without any interruption. The "informational", on which everything "physical" or "material" is based in principle, now strives to proceed infinitely and without limits.
It possesses a kind of *"ethereal"* equivalent. Every kind of life, which once began on the "physical side" due to the formation of sufficiently

advanced spiritual or informational clusters, proceeds now in a new and different form.

Near-death experiences (NDEs) show that the people concerned perceive themselves as being "physically still undamaged", although their "previous – physical – body" just then is undergoing reanimation at the scene of an accident or on the operating table.

This seems to me to be a very clear indication that there is probably indeed a kind of "ethereal body" which continues on a different level. However, our "coarse, physical sensory organs" or other physical devices cannot perceive it. Therefore, the term "ethereal", usually used in esoteric context, seems to be very apt.

At the moment of death *(here* symbolised as interface 1) the "informational part" (-1) of a person, or in other words, his personality, has reached the maximum level of complexity.

Its existence now continues in an "ethereal body" (+1) which is no longer perceptible to our senses.

People tend to polarise. If you are asked in a discussion as to how life continues after death, hardly anyone understands you when you answer, "I do not know 'how' exactly, but it will go on".

And we do not come back here either, as many followers in some religions and esoteric circles imagine: we will thus not be "reincarnated in the flesh". Often they then bring forward many arguments: They say that there are allegedly so many children giving authentic reports of recognising environments and families, that there are exact sightings or even that they are able to speak foreign languages during so-called regression hypnoses. Surely that should be enough evidence. Then they do not want to understand that I do not doubt some phenomena, but that I consider their interpretation to be wrong. Everything can also be explained on the basis of elementary mathematical logic.

The world in which we live in the "here and now" is not only the one, the physical world, but from the very beginning also the "other", the informational and spiritual world. This is clearly proven by the fact that we can live and think at all and that we thereby perceive continuity, which continues for us in space and time.

None of this exists in the physical, material world.

So they do indeed exist, the many parallel worlds as mathematics suggests once again. However, they are different from those envisaged by many cosmologists and science fiction authors.

The depiction of the Yin and Yang symbol (cf. Fig. 1 and 8) in a circle, where the black and white flames face each other and "inspire each other", is also applicable to the manifested evolution of everything in the world.

However, in this case the circle, the symbol for the origin of evolution with perfection in unity, soon turns into a square as a new perfection in multiplicity (cf. my intellectual game in Fig. 2).

If we now take this as the symbol of evolution, then the two flames "spirit" and "matter" become synonyms for the "informational" (spirit) and the "physical world" (matter). And with every step of actual life, let us say from conception to birth, then a new step from birth to so-called death, and thereafter many more "linearly upward" striving lives further, the "informational" or "spiritual" part inherent in all of us increases steadily

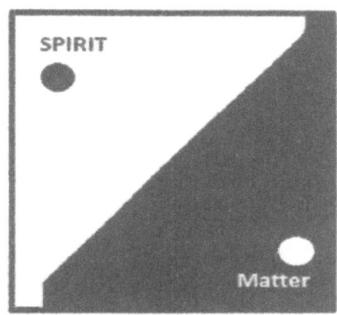

Fig. 14: The principle of evolution analogous to Yin and Yang in Chinese philosophy

and the "physical" part decreases or grows more ethereal (Fig. 14). This also ties in very well with the upward development of the Riemann spiral (cf. Fig. 11).

But this also renders it invisible from a "coarse physical" point of view; for how should we be able to perceive it sensually?

Nevertheless, we can definitely *experience* it, some of us better than others. However, this belongs then to the ECEs, the *extraordinary consciousness experiences*. But then we have to allow them to happen. Yet this is precisely what most people do not want to do.

Death is merely an interface which can be derived with elementary mathematical logic. But since the same logic obviously seems to regulate everything important, this analogy seems to be very apt here.

After all, it encompasses, contains and thus explains a great many phenomena, which are rejected by traditional natural sciences, so, among others, also those phenomena which are associated with reincarnation and are supposed to contribute to its alleged proof.

The world awaiting us after death can hardly be described in our words, simply because we do not have words for it.
Just as little could embryos describe what is awaiting them after birth before they are born – if they were theoretically able to do so. However, this different and new world is far from being a purely "spiritual world" or a pure "world of information" devoid of any "physical matter". It is just more "ethereal" than the world we had previously experienced and to which we had been accustomed.

Images of "angels in white robes with no real substance", just floating around, are likely to be just as wrong. We continue to perceive ourselves as an intact and complete person with all the attributes of our personality which has matured up to this moment we call "death". This includes all the good, but also all the bad sides of our personality. We will still benefit from the good ones which will continue to help us in the further process. For the bad ones we will have to take over responsibility. And if they led us to commit great injustice to other people in the "here and now", or if we have caused them harm, then we will have to expiate every single case, unless we have already done so here and forgiveness has been granted. So, we must ask everyone for forgiveness. We will also receive it at some point, since both to grant forgiveness and to ask for forgiveness are the essential prerequisites for our own advancement – for each single one of us.

"Extraordinary consciousness experiences (ECEs)", including especially NDEs, indicate this again and again with various contents. Numerous people have been reporting them since time immemorial and testify to them despite threats of torture and death.

ECEs in general (and especially NDEs) also seem to me to be simultaneously the basis and the trellis for very many legends and myths, but ultimately also for all religions.

Thus, the fundamental principles of elementary mathematical logic and its basic geometric forms, which I have repeatedly put forward and made use of since my first two books published in 1999, and which are completely independent of any calculation system, deliver an excellent *"red thread"*.

It is thus possible in every situation and for every level to calculate what could be and what will rather not be, or else, how it should be and how rather not and, if it could be, then also, why.

What seems to be expected how and when?

The figure below gives a good initial overview:

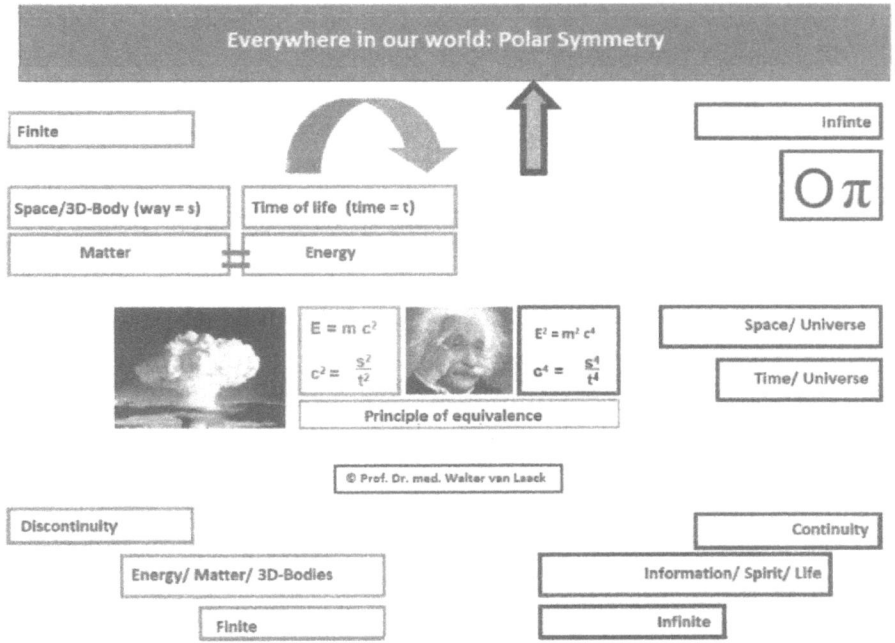

Fig. 15: Polar symmetry everywhere, further explanations in the text below

There are two polar-symmetrical, i.e. mirror-inverted and simultaneously oppositional sides in this world. However, they cannot be considered separately, but they rather influence each other and merge to some extent (cf. Fig. 14).

In the course of immense periods of time the "informational" side grows ever more pronounced and dominant. In contrast, the material, physical part of the whole recedes more and more into the background. In any case, everything physical, everything material is, above all, a means to an end:

In the long run, it serves the evolution of the informational, hence mainly the spiritual.

In our "current world", or, as I like to term it, in the "here and now", the "physical part" of the world still very much dominates.

Informational contents become perceptible only if they are being approached by someone's spirit – or with *reason* according to *Kant*.

Then the *reality of infinity* becomes recognisable, which does not exist in physics, hence also no infinite space, which, however, according to *Albert Einstein*, really describes our universe.

And we recognise that, although we experience our lives as a *continuum* and time passes *continuously for us*, *neither* can be a phenomenon of the physical world, since that is exclusively the world of the *discontinuous* and thus of *quantisation*.

Physics knows the *principle of equivalence* as established by Albert Einstein: Matter and energy are two sides of the same coin and thus "equivalent". This means that they can be transformed into each other.

Unfortunately, the atomic bomb has demonstrated that an immense amount of energy can be created from a small amount of matter. Almost everyone today has heard of Einstein's famous equation (see Fig. 15). But here the *mass "m"* means the rest mass, for example, of atoms. However, does it exist in practice? No, it does not. This is pure theory.

In practice, the universe is always dynamic, as are all the particles within it. For dynamic processes, the Einstein equation must also be "dynamised". In mathematics, this means that it must be squared. This creates a new equation, which is also found in Fig. 15, it is written to the right side of the known one on the left. However, the smallest particles such as photons themselves are also *interfaces* between the two worlds of "matter" and "information", since they have no rest mass. In the equation on the right hand side of Fig. 15, depicting the dynamic universe, the *speed of light "c"* is now raised to the fourth power. Velocity is physically *"distance divided by time"*. Both are, therefore, raised to the fourth power. This indicates unequivocally that our concept of a four-dimensional space-time must be wrong. Einstein's equation is correct, but some interpretations are thus probably incorrect.

As previously mentioned, *Peter Plichta* already proposed a *really existing, four-dimensional space* in the 1990s and he envisaged it as two interlocking, infinite planes. I gratefully took up his suggestion in my first book published in 1999. Still in 1999, I was *the first* to develop a completely new thought model and several new mathematical approaches and have since explained them in numerous books.

They depict coherent analogies for the emergence of our world and all further developments (Figs. 2, 10 and 15 to 19).

The conception of a real 4D space would correspond exactly with what we actually see, regardless of where and how far we look: Everywhere, cosmic space is flat and level or, as we also label it, planar or Euclidian[34], i.e. probably not curved.

The notion that smallest particles – such as photons of light – can be "bent" by strong gravitational forces emitted by large objects such as the Sun, is simply based on the fact that *gravitation and light are two polar-symmetrical effects exerted on each other,* but not on an assumed curvature of space. The phenomenon does exist indeed, but the common interpretation seems to be incorrect once again.

By the way, we also arrive at a *genuine* four-dimensional space if we just proceed logically with my thought model (see Fig. 2 as well as

---

[34] According to Euclid of Alexandria, Greek mathematician, who probably lived in the 3rd century B.C.

numerous detailed explanations in some of my books): My thought model shows a development which starts with a circle (C1), with its circumference and area depicting *infinity*. The circle is *clearly defined* by three *informational coordinates* from an "informational world". After only a few steps we arrive at *four* circles (C1-C4). This opens up the second level, the plane (from Fig. 2 to Fig. 16).

Starting from a *unity* (the circle C1 with "incorporated infinity") we arrive at a first, new perfection in *multiplicity* with the square (S) which only shows finiteness. The process is determined solely by a logical procedure. Along the path, we will detect crucial cornerstones and parameters of this world (Fig. 16).

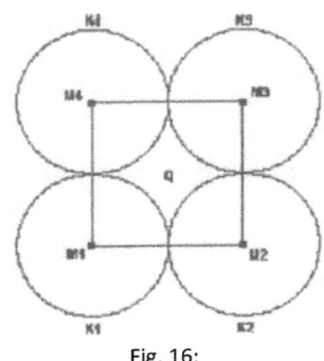

Fig. 16:

So, what is the next logical step to take? We have to raise the plane in order to develop *space* next. This gives us two *planes* controlled by *two* ordinal numbers, depicted here by number circles with arrows pointing outwards (Fig. 17). Both planes are perpendicular to each other.

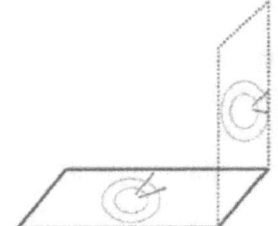

Fig. 17:

Both surfaces then penetrate each other infinitely according to the formula x^2y^2 and thus form a flat, level or Euclidean space, that of our real universe. It is infinite (Fig. 18).

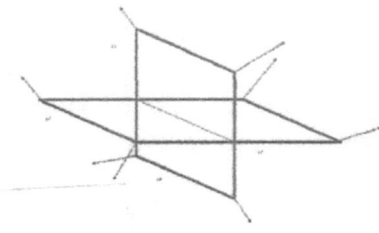

Fig. 18:

Just like space, which is now raised to the fourth power (Fig. 15), together with the unit for distance (s) in the dynamised Einstein

102

equation, so must time (t), of course, also exist as being raised to the *fourth power* and must consequently also be four-dimensional itself.
I have already discussed this repeatedly in other books. However, this would take matters too far here and, therefore, I kindly ask for your understanding and refer you to my earlier books.

It is the spirit of this world which has evidently started out to strive for the greatest possible perfection in maximum diversity.
Or, as the French theologian and philosopher *Teilhard de Chardin (1881-1955)* expressed it so beautifully: *"Are we not all together a God in the making?"*
I think he is right.

Therefore, it must be pointed out time and again that the development of the world does not aim for collectivism which some contemporaries currently once again like to stylise as the symbol of their social ideas. In doing so, they once again commit a crime against humanity, possibly for years or even decades to come, since they do not seem to be willing or able to understand the core of the whole.

The world strives for the highest perfection in greatest diversity.
It relies rigorously on individuality with no ifs or buts.
The individual alone is important. Only if all individuals contribute to this growth and are prepared to take their neighbour on board, only then can and will the highest perfection be achieved at some point.
Those of us who are already on a higher level of informational growth must not treat the weaker ones in a top-down fashion and exclude them. *They must be taken along.* The currently widespread "elitism" of some contemporaries will mainly cause themselves the biggest trouble "some day" if they do not already in the "here and now" repent in spirit and action.
For them, the words of the evangelist *and* Apostle *Matthew (19:30)* should be a warning: "... the last will be first" – and vice versa.

Everything falls into place perfectly

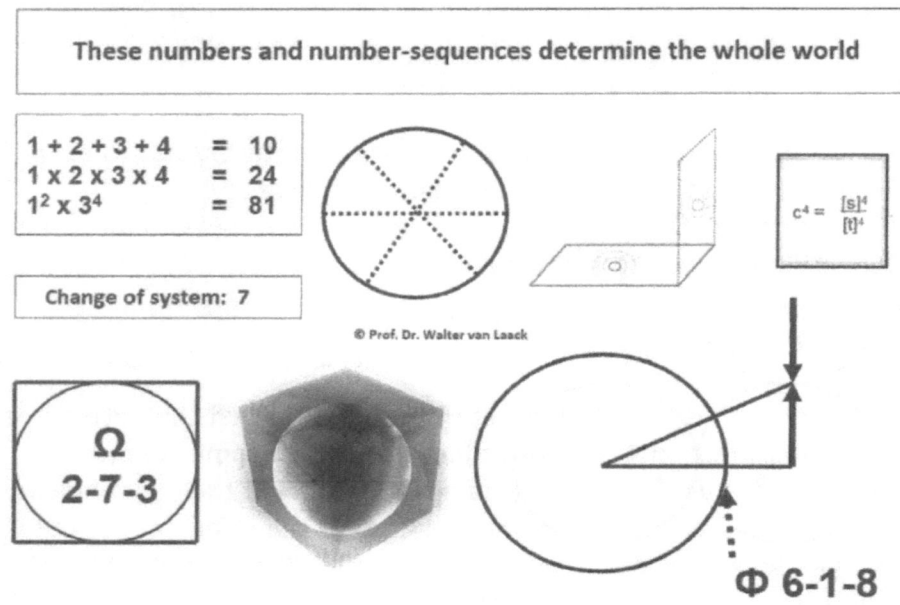

These numbers and number-sequences determine the whole world

$$1 + 2 + 3 + 4 = 10$$
$$1 \times 2 \times 3 \times 4 = 24$$
$$1^2 \times 3^4 = 81$$

Change of system: 7

$$c^4 = \frac{[s]^4}{[t]^4}$$

© Prof. Dr. Walter van Laack

$$\Omega$$
$$2\text{-}7\text{-}3$$

$$\Phi \ 6\text{-}1\text{-}8$$

Fig. 19: These numbers and sequences determine the world. See also the text below.

I have already explained almost all the numerical relationships in the diagram above (Fig. 19). Out of pure information, in the sense of spatial coordinates, the smallest *finite point, a circle,* emerged, which represents simultaneously the smallest "material" form or physical *unity.*

With this initial circle, all the important basic geometries of our world could be developed after only a few steps by means of an ingeniously simple intellectual model, up to a first new perfection in *multiplicity,* the square. With the square, a number structuring via the first four ordinal numbers is completed. Since a circle can be structured by means of natural numbers and fractions up to the number 6, it already contains 6 equilateral triangles right at the beginning.

Since the square, as the first perfection in the new multiplicity, arises from the centres of the starting circles, now multiplied to four, the structural number 24 arises simultaneously via 4 x 6.

This in turn is also the product of the first 4 ordinal numbers by which it is formed, thus 1 x 2 x 3 x 4 = 24.

Since after a division by 7 it is no longer possible to depict the result with natural numbers (ordinal numbers), the number 7 represents a caesura.

On a large as well as on a small scale, everything in this world above 10^7, i.e. the sum of the first 4 ordinal numbers raised to the power of 7, can be found in a completely new form. In between there is predominantly "empty space".

So, the number 7, representing a caesura, probably always indicates a system change. If we start at 10^0 metres, i.e. 1 metre, then we look at the Earth at 10^7 metres, at $10^{2 \times 7}$ metres we look at our solar system and at $10^{3 \times 7}$ metres we look at our milky way. $10^{4 \times 7}$ meters is still unknown to us. That is still far beyond the possibilities of our sensory perception: even the best telescopes of this world cannot even nearly reach that far.

If we turn to the "small" things, we first arrive at 10^{-7} metres and look at our chromosomes and their genes. At $10^{-2 \times 7}$ metres we already look at atomic nuclei with their nuclear particles. And that is also the limit for us at present. Of course, this does not mean that we could not (in theory) look infinitely further. However, even with the necessary technical add-ons and new inventions would we then again only be able to perceive a finite number of further infinitesimally small particles with our senses.[35]

I have already gone into detail explaining other important aspects of my illustration above, such as the necessary dynamisation of Einstein's equation, enabling us to discover the true nature of this world, the important number sequences 6-1-8 of the "Golden Section ϕ" and 2-7-3

---

[35] See also the wonderful "picture book" by P. Morrison and P. Morrison "Powers of Ten: About the Relative Size of Things in the Universe" (1994)

for the "limit of (physical) feasibility Ω" as I have termed it. Taken together, this leads irrevocably to the conclusion that all physical matter in our world possesses inherent information which develops in the same way as the external physical part, i.e. it is also subject to its own separate evolution. However, eventually, there comes the point when the informational evolution will differentiate from the evolution of physical matter. It soon proceeds faster, and this will eventually lead to an eminent and visible divergence, both qualitatively and quantitatively.

In this context I would, therefore, like to refer to the *first four ordinal numbers* again. Evidently, they bear a tremendously important and determining function:

We should accept that the world "calculates" in the decimal system. In the course or human history, 16 out of 20 major cultures have adopted this for practical reasons. The number 10 is the sum of the first four ordinal numbers, i.e. $1 + 2 + 3 + 4 = 10$.

Modern cultures, which have not yet followed this path, may, simply due to this fact, remain unable to recognise our world correctly, because they probably cannot see the wood for the trees.

In numerous religions and myths the number 24 seems to play an important role, just as it does also in physics. It is the product of the first four ordinal numbers: $1 \times 2 \times 3 \times 4 = 24$.

As I have already mentioned, it also results from the 6 equilateral triangles in each of the first four circles (C1-4) in my thought model. It is the structuring number of these circles.

All prime numbers, which are only divisible by 1 and by themselves, follow the equation $6n\pm1$. Here, "n" stands for all consecutive ordinal numbers. If $n = 4$, the result is 24. This is the first number around which no accompanying *prime twins* exist. As "n" grows, these soon appear less and less frequently. Up to the number 18 (for $n = 3$) they appear regularly, e.g. $n = 1$ i.e. 6 is accompanied by the prime numbers 5 and 7, $n = 2$, i.e. 12, is accompanied by the prime numbers 11 and 13, and $n = 3$, i.e. 18, is accompanied by the two prime numbers 17 and 19. These are called prime twins. With the number 4 as the last of the first four ordinal numbers this regularity comes to an end.

The number 24 seems to be a very important and constant feature for the structuring of the entire universal space. Therefore, it is a crucial "space structure constant".

In my earlier books I have already described and explained in detail that the "structuring of space" follows the same logic: Thus, starting from the *first* circle in my "intellectual model of creation" (fig. 2) soon three further circles will develop. As the first of these four the others will also be structured by the number 6 (making 6 equilateral triangles), (i.e. 4 x 6 = 24). Further number circles around all can then be generated towards the outside. In doing so, the number 24 is multiplied by the numerical value of each further circle: Circumcircle 2 results in 2 x 24 = 48, circumcircle 3 then results in 3 x 24 = 72 and so on. In this way, an informational space is again and again newly created around each new "finite BEING", e.g. around each new piece of matter. Thus, the world fulfills again its inherent aspiration of highest possible perfection in maximum diversity. This applies to everything, to every living being such as humans, as well as to every single new atom of all "finite objects". *Each of these spaces is purely informational and infinite.*

The informational space around every finite body is encoded by numbers and grows circularly and further and further – just like ripples in water when you throw a stone into a pond.

This numerical code must then, of course, also be based on the foundations of my thought model. Around each new BEING, number circles are generated which are structured by the number 24.

In this circular development of infinite spaces, which are of purely informational nature and thus infinite, the prime numbers also play a very important role. Unfortunately, an even further detailed description of all these interrelations would once more go beyond the scope of this book, so that I recommend again some books of my book list below.[36]

---

[36] ... and especially my book "To Perceive The World With Logic". (English edition 2007)

There is, however, a third number which also consists of the first four ordinal numbers and which has evidently also very great importance: *It is the number 81.*

If we were to describe it with the first four ordinal numbers, the whole miracle of this world is revealed at once: It unequivocally points out to us clearly that information is involved everywhere. The smallest unit of information is the number 1.

So far, we have used two basic arithmetic operations to arrive at absolutely crucial parameters: The addition of the first 4 natural numbers results in 10, the multiplication of these 4 numbers results in the number 24. The next higher arithmetic operation is squaring. Its reverse arithmetic operation is the root extraction (square root extraction) which has already been discussed. The number 81 indeed results from 3^4, i.e. with the aid of only two of the first 4 ordinal numbers. *However, this again means that we do not see the wood for the trees. Why is that?*

The number 1 must be involved since this is the information, which is inherent in all "BEING". My simple "intellectual model of creation" started by drawing on a plane, i.e. in two dimensions, mathematically: xy. The apparently infinite cosmic space seems to have a *real four-dimensionality,* as already explained: x^2y^2. The information "1" for all BEING must, therefore, be squared. *The result is: 1^2.*

Consequently, for all important and naturally occurring non-disintegrating "things", "materials" or, in general, "substances", we find the number $81 = 1^2 \times 3^4$. Once again, this value is also generated by the first 4 natural numbers (ordinal numbers).

Two examples from Chemistry and Biology

1) Chemistry: In the entire universe there are exactly 81 naturally occurring and non-disintegrating (non-radioactive) elements. In traditional teaching the periodic table always shows 83 elements: however, element 43 (technetium) and element 61 (promethium) are radioactive, although they occur naturally.

2) Biology: the genetic code consists of nucleic acids which occur as long nucleic acid chains. In the cell nuclei, they are found as double-stranded DNA, fragmented in the form of chromosomes.
We could also say that the entire DNA, also termed genome, is equivalent to a multivolume encyclopaedia and each chromosome represents just one volume. The cell nucleus is like a safe and keeps the treasure secure. There are also single-stranded nucleic acids chains termed RNA. In the context of the Corona virus crisis, one of them, the so-called mRNA (messenger RNA) caused something of a stir, because it acts as a messenger between the encyclopaedia in the cell nucleus and the production sites for proteins, the building materials of every living body on Earth, in the cell.
The genetic code works with 4 letters A, G, C and T in the DNA and U instead of T in the RNA.[37] These letters stand for 4 substances, called bases. These are always arranged in threes with the aid of sugar and phosphoric acid. The whole is termed nucleotide and the arrangement of three bases with a supplement is called a "triplet" or a codon. This is the equivalent of a "genetic word".
Biologists constructed a 4^3-code already some time ago, based on the number 4 for the number of genetic letters and the number 3 for their arrangement in the triplet: According to them, there would be $4^3 = 64$ possibilities for assembling the 20 essential amino acids (AA), which occur in nature, into proteins, as the code sun (Fig. 20) below shows. It follows that the code would be "hopelessly oversized". That is why it is

---

[37] These are the so-called bases adenine, guanine, cytosine and thymine in DNA, and uracil in RNA.

called "degenerated". For me, this makes the remains of my hair stand on end, since, in my experience throughout life, nature is never degenerated but it is rather the scientists who may often be before they discover the truth.

As we know today, this applies to the 95% of "genetic rubbish", as it was termed up until a few years ago, and this also applies to the assumption that the genetic code is degenerated: In the second volume "Life" of my three-volume book series "A Better History of Our World" I was *the first person ever* to point out, back in 2001, that in fact the exact inversion of this "genetic code" is probably correct, i.e. *not* $4^3 = 64$, *but*: $3^4 = 81$.

Now it becomes clear to everyone that the same mathematical rules seem to apply at a key position in biology as everywhere else in the entire universe. *But why now 3^4?*

No, it is by no means arbitrary, just to accommodate some idea.

On the contrary, the idea that $3^4 = 81$ is the right choice for the genetic code is already evident in the same well-known code sun (Fig. 20). It even enhances the genetic code considerably, it now turns into a "placeholder code": It allocates each base, and hence each nucleotide, to a specifically defined location in the order of the words, and thus in each chapter.

Consequently, the genetic code is effectively protected against incidental damage, such as random mutations, for example. Each AA is assigned to its own place. If the sequence is out of order, it is now immediately detectable. As a reminder: A nucleotide transports an amino acid (AA), which is in a gene what a letter is in a word. Here is an example: *Cytochrome C* is a particularly important enzyme in the respiratory system. The protein consists of 104 amino acids. Even up to 70 of these could be exchanged without any damage being caused.

We know something similar from a language experiment: Please try to read the following text as fluently as possible:

Tihs magssee sowhs waht oru biarn is cablepa of. Ralley amizang! Acicodring to a unervitsy sudty, it deos not mettar in wchih ordre teh lertets aer in a wodr.

Written correctly it says: This message shows what our brain is capable of. Really amazing! According to a university study, it does not matter in which order the letters are in a word.

In order not to get everything mixed up, the genetic code defines the respective locations precisely:

By means of *four* organic bases, which are always arranged in *threes* as codons (nucleotide triplets), all 20 amino acids (α-AA), which are assembled in biological bodies to proteins, can be encoded. Several triplets can

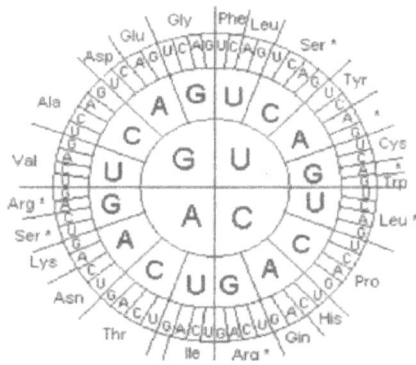

Fig. 20: Genetic "Code Sun"

also determine one and the same AA. For example, 9 AAs are linked by two triplets in each case.

In the end there are 84 possibilities. But does this not contradict the 3^4 code for 81 "seats"? No it does not, because in fact there are 3 "nonsense triplets". They always lie at the end of a reading process and do not carry an AA. This leaves 81 triplets which transport an amino acid and this is exactly right.

And at this point, something else must be mentioned: The genetic code always contains one triplet which starts a reading process, the start codon.

So it is of tremendous importance. This means that there are indeed 81 places, but *one place* is of outstanding significance and it always indicates the start.

At this point let us briefly return to *chemistry*: There are 81 chemical elements in the entire universe, which are stable and which occur naturally. *One* element in particular stands out: it is the first, *hydrogen H*. It is the most widely spread element in the entire cosmos.

Mathematics provides us with proof for the very subtle "dualism" only occurring on the informational level between the two worlds, the "informational" and the "physical" world.

Immanuel Kant once said: *"The entire nature is actually nothing other than an interrelation of phenomena in accordance with rules."*

Endless Consciousness?

Recently, at the end of a long video interview, I was asked by the editor, whether everything is perhaps "endless consciousness".[38] She seemed to have come across this term because my colleague *van Lommel in* The Netherlands published his book in *2008* under this title which has been marketed successfully in several languages.

In fact, however, I already postulated, presented and explained this idea in great detail much earlier – in my first two books, published in German, in 1999. The second book was released in English shortly afterwards in 2000.[39]

Yes, consciousness is indeed endless. And not only that. It is also eternal.

But not everything endless and eternal is also consciousness.

This is rather a currently widespread esoteric assumption.

As you should know by now after having read this book, "infinity" and "eternity" are *properties of "information"*, but not of matter. They are not physical concepts.

---

[38] Video interview by BILD (German daily newspaper) on 05.03.2021

[39] "Plädoyer für ein Leben nach dem Tod und eine etwas andere Sicht der Welt" (1999 not available in English) and "Key To Eternity" (2000). The English edition has ever since been available internationally.

Mainly in esoteric concepts it is propagated that all life originates from an "endless consciousness" and returns to it. Such concepts tend to be based on the currently fashionable approach of collectivist thinking: According to these ideas, our individuality would be pure illusion already in the "here and now", and after our death it would disintegrate completely. Only a kind of essence of it would remain as a (collective) soul. Finally, it would continue to exist like a drop in water within an indivisible and indissoluble whole. If not immediately then soon, it would be without any memory of or connection to the previous life in the "here and now", as I like to call it.

Everything would just fall into oblivion.

Those who "believe in reincarnation"[40] envisage the deceased "soul" – usually already without memory of the previous life and after a certain time "in waiting" – on its way into a new carnal body, some of them always into a human body, but others also into those of other forms of life.

I consider all such concepts to be myths, religions and pseudo-religions or esotericism – whatever suits – *but not to be the truth.*

Of course, there are differences and contradictions among all these groups. Many also reject such ideas altogether. This is why I will once again refer to what I just said:

Although consciousness is endless and eternal, it must nevertheless have come into existence at some point. *It has not always been there.*

In accordance with the elementary mathematical rules and regularities which I have outlined here, "information" emerges initially from "i" – represented by the negative numbers.

Consciousness is not a static product – and it is even less a collective one. *Consciousness is a purely individual and already advanced level of the development of information.*

However, once consciousness has emerged, it will continue to evolve incessantly.

---

[40] Although the belief in reincarnation goes back to late Hindu scriptures, the term "reincarnation" was only coined by the French spiritualist Allan Kardec (1804-1869) as late as 1857.

Consciousness is always a property of an already highly complex "information cluster" – as I call it.

This means that consciousness in this universe is always a property of an already higher developed living being.

Other physical entities certainly possess "information", but this does not at all mean that they possess consciousness.

Life is a basic prerequisite necessary for the emergence of consciousness. As I have already explained, life itself is a property of the "informational part of the world".

This means that the developmental stage "life" precedes the stage "consciousness". *Only something alive can also develop consciousness.*

But should death then not end consciousness? *Not at all!* Since what we call "death" is by no means the end of advanced spiritual or, generally speaking, of informational complexity.

The ability of living beings to develop consciousness remains intact in the form they have *individually* generated and developed previously, even after death. Life or Spirit, & Consciousness and so on: It is all ultimately "information".

We call the growing "information cluster" of a person "his/her personality" and, at the time of death, "his/her soul".

Although this is something purely individual, it is nevertheless also part of a whole, since information is divisible and yet coherent, just like a sequence of numbers.

Information has continuity, whereas physics only knows discontinuity or quantisation.

Although culture represents a collective state of development, it has only been enabled to develop up to that level and will continue to do so successfully if as many of its individuals as possible develop *themselves* further – and, in the best case, even all of them. *Only then does the cultural level also grow.*

Many people see this in a different way and unfortunately their view is mostly blurred by ideological lenses. *However, they are wrong,* and, as

114

a result, they harm their fellow human beings who voluntarily follow them or who are entrusted to them and unfortunately, above all, those who are subjugated by them – often lastingly and for a very long time. However, they will all come to regret this behaviour very much one day.

As I have already explained, consciousness is a higher property of the first really experienceable world, the "informational world".
Ordinal numbers and simple geometric forms are also its basis and constitute the framework – or the informational scaffolding – for the physical world which is generated together with it and which emerges from it.
Self-awareness is already a small step higher than "mere" consciousness, and life is the prerequisite for developing these two higher qualities in the first place. A lifeless stone will never have consciousness – yet it is full of information.
However, all forms of consciousness are just stages of a very different evolution than the only one we think we know.
It is an evolution which most people have undoubtedly overlooked up till now or which they have not even considered. All forms of consciousness are stages in an evolution of the spiritual or, in general, in an evolution of the "informational".

The evolution of the spiritual is – from our point of view – endless and eternal.
All properties which emerge and then develop further along this path are simultaneously eternally compatible downwards and, of course, they are also retained forever, but not, as in physics, only as smallest, indivisible, discontinuous particles.
No, they remain always preserved in their continuity as well as in their acquired complexity.
Accordingly, consciousness is also, of course, endless, but only part of the whole. And, as already explained, not everything endless is consciousness.

The evolution of the spiritual or, in general, the "informational world" is the ultimate goal and for this purpose the world needs the physical side as a means to an end.

This can also be found analogously in the *Riemann spiral* (Fig. 11), named in reference to the German mathematician *Bernhard Riemann (1826-1866).*

The essence of this world, the "informational side", continually creates and structures itself anew with the constant aid of the "physical side", and drives the development ceaselessly and *linearly* upwards – towards ever higher perfection in ever greater diversity.

Everything taken together seems to be, as *Teilhard de Chardin* once expressed it so beautifully, "a God in the making".

It depends on us alone to shape this development successfully with all our strength – and thus with love and responsibility for ourselves and our neighbours – in the "divine sense". Then we ourselves will benefit most from this development on this still very long path.

Every one of us should become aware of this.

Books by Prof. Dr. Walter van Laack currently available in English:

1. Novel:

Our Key To Eternity
ISBN 978-3-936624-18-2 (SC), 308 p. (2016)
ISBN 978-3-936624-31-1, E-Book (2016)

2. Non-fiction Books

GREATER THAN THE ENTIRE UNIVERSE
ISBN 978-3-936624-52-6, (SC) 120 p. (2022)
ISBN 978-3-936624-54-0, E-Book (2022)

Non-Fiction-Book-Series: "Keystones Of Our World"
Vol 1: The Whole World Is Information
ISBN 978-3-936624-33-5 (SC), 68 p. (2016)
ISBN 978-3-936624-34-2, E-Book (2016)

To Perceive The World With Logic
ISBN 978-3-936624-08-3, Softcover (SC), 340 p. (2007)
ISBN 978-3-936624-09-0, E-Book (2008)

Nobody Ever Dies!
ISBN 978-3-936624-03-8, (SC), 272 p. (2005)
ISBN 978-3-936624-22-9, E-Book (2013)
A Better History of Our World
Vol. 1, "The Universe"
ISBN 978-3-8311-1490-0, (SC), 188 p. (2001)
Vol. 2, "Life"
ISBN 978-3-8311-2597-5, (SC), 236 p. (2002)
Vol. 3, "Death"
ISBN 978-3-936624-01-4, (SC), 276 p. (2003)
Key To Eternity
ISBN 978-3-8311-0344-7, (SC), 256 p. (2000)

3. "Lectures & Insights"

**World views yesterday and today – What will remain and
what will be laughed at tomorrow?"**
ISBN 978-3-936624-47-2. 56 p. (2020)

Dying and Death from a Scientific Point of View –
Sterben und Tod aus wissenschaftlicher Sicht
(Upside-Down Book)
ISBN 978-3-936624-41-0, Softcover (SC), 44 p. (2018)
ISBN 978-3-936624-42-7, E-book (2018)

Books by Prof. Dr. Walter van Laack currently available in German:

1. Novel:

Unser Schlüssel zur Ewigkeit
ISBN 978-3-936624-16-8, Paperback (SC), 316 p. (2015)
ISBN 978-3-936624-27-4, E-Book (2015)

2. Nonfiction books

GRÖßER ALS DAS GANZE UNIVERSUM
ISBN 978-3-936624-38-0, (SC) 120 p. (2021)

Mit Logik die Welt begreifen
ISBN 978-3-936624-04-5, Paperback (SC), 380 p. (2005)
ISBN 978-3-936624-07-6, Hardcover (HC), 380 p. (2005)
ISBN 978-3-936624-23-6, E-Book (2013)

Wer stirbt, ist nicht tot!
ISBN 978-3-936624-12-0, (SC), 272 p. (New edition 2011)
ISBN 978-3-936624-13-7, (HC), 272 p. (New edition 2011)
ISBN 978-3-936624-21-2, E-Book (2013)

Eine bessere Geschichte unserer Welt
Volume 1, "Das Universum"
ISBN 978-3-8311-0345-4, (SC), 196 p. (2000)
Volume 2, "Das Leben"
ISBN 978-3-8311-2114-4, (SC), 248 p., (2001)
Volume 3, "Der Tod"
ISBN 978-3-8311-3581-3, (SC), 276 p. (2002)

Der Schlüssel zur Ewigkeit
ISBN 978-3-9805239-4-3, (HC), 288 p., First edition (1999)
ISBN 978-3-89811-819-4, (SC), 288 p., Second edition (2000)

Plädoyer für ein Leben nach dem Tod und eine etwas andere Sicht der Welt
ISBN 978-3-89811-818-7; (SC), 448 p., second edition (1999/2000)

3. "Lectures & Insights"

Weltbilder gestern und heute – Was bleibt und worüber lacht man morgen?
ISBN 978-3-936624-44-1 , Paperback (SC), German, 56 p. (2019)

**Sterben und Tod aus wissenschaftlicher Sicht –
Dying and Death from a Scientific Point of View**
(Upside-Down book)
ISBN 978-3-36624-41-0, Paperback (SC), German & English, 44 p. (2018)
ISBN 978-3-936624-42-7, E-Book (2018)

4. Conference Transcript series „Schnittstelle Tod"

Was lernen wir durch Corona über Leben und Tod?
ISBN 978-3-936624-55-7, Paperback (SC), (2022)
Aufbruch oder Ende, Kontakte oder Hirngespinste?
ISBN 978-3-936624-51-9, Paperback (SC), 164 p. (2020)
Sind Religionen religiös und Wissenschaften wissend?
ISBN 978-3-936624-36-6, Paperback (SC), 172 p. (2018)
Wo stehen wir nach 40 Jahren NTE-Forschung?
ISBN 978-3-936624-30-4, Paperback (SC), 92 p., (2016)
Was spricht für unser Weiterleben?
ISBN 978-3-936624-19-9, Paperback (SC), 100 p., (2014)
Warum auf ein Danach vertrauen?
ISBN 978-3-936624-14-4, Paperback (SC), 120 p., (2012)
Aufbruch zu neuem Leben?
ISBN 978-3-936624-10-6, Paperback (SC), 148 p., (2010)

van Laack GmbH, Aachen, Germany, Publishing House
(HRB-Aachen 5584)
CEO: Prof. Dr. Walter van Laack
Shareholders:
Dr.-Ing. Dipl.-Wirt.-Ing. Alexander van Laack,
Martin van Laack, M.Sc.,
Prof. Dr. med. Walter van Laack

Roermonder Str. 312, D-52072 Aachen, Germany
Fax: +49(0)3212-9319310 - Email: webmaster@van-Laack.de
Web: www.vanLaack-Buch.de - www.Nahtoderfahrung.info

Sales exclusively by: BoD, Books-on-Demand
In de Tarpen 42, D-22848 Norderstedt, Germany   Fax +49(0)40-534335-84,
Email: info@bod.de   -   Web: www.bod.de